Towards a World War III Scenario

Michel Chossudovsky exposes the insanity of our privatized war machine. Iran is being targeted with nuclear weapons as part of a war agenda built on distortions and lies for the purpose of private profit. The real aims are oil, financial hegemony and global control. The price could be nuclear holocaust. When weapons become the hottest export of the world's only superpower, and diplomats work as salesmen for the defense industry, the whole world is recklessly endangered. If we must have a military, it belongs entirely in the public sector. No one should profit from mass death and destruction.

-Ellen Brown, author of *Web of Debt* and president of the Public Banking Institute

The current global economic meltdown, with no solution in sight, makes imperialism shed its liberal-democratic cloak and openly declare pre-emptive nuclear war as its essential military doctrine and praxis.

-Admiral Vishnu Bhagwat, former Chief of India's Naval Staff

Once again, Michel Chossudovsky helps us understand what is really going on.

-David Ray Griffin, Professor of Theology and author of *9/11 Ten Years Later*

The vast historical tapestry that the author reveals appears at a crucial moment when we are faced with the stark choice of war and peace. The inestimable value of this short and superb work is that it does not compromise in its robust affirmation of the truth and its profound belief that forms of exploitation and injustice, wherever they may be found, must be fought.

-Frederick Clairmonte, distinguished economist and author of 1960s classic, *The Rise and Fall of Economic Liberalism: The Making of the Economic Gulag*

This detailed and highly documented book is essential reading at a critical time in history. In it, Dr. Chossudovsky unveils a startling analysis of the new policy for the actual use of nuclear weapons as "instruments of peace" on countries such as Iran and North Korea. The media grants legitimacy to these "pre-emptive military actions" for self-defense, portraying the perpetrators, who are engaged in a profit-driven agenda for global dominance, as victims of evil in the "clash of civilizations".

-Elizabeth Woodworth, author of *The November Deep*

Michel Chossudovsky's book "Towards a World War III Scenario: The Dangers of Nuclear War" should be read by "The 1% of the World Population".

-Pablo Gonzalez Casanova, Professor of Sociology, Autonomous University of Mexico

The "mutually assured destruction" of nuclear war is laid out in the US military's plan, already underway, to modernize the nuclear stockpile for use on the other side of the world, as if blowback doesn't exist. The message is clear: nuclear states are the real terrorists in today's world; the antiwar movement must unite with antinuke activists and together uphold 9/11 truth.

-Rady Ananda, prominent author and biotechnology analyst

Towards a World War III Scenario

The Dangers of Nuclear War

Michel Chossudovsky

Global Research

Towards a World War III Scenario. The Dangers of Nuclear War

by Michel Chossudovsky

© Michel Chossudovsky, 2012. All rights reserved – Global Research Publishers, Centre for Research on Globalization (CRG).

No part of this book may be used or reproduced in any manner whatsoever without written permission of the publisher.

Global Research Publishers is a division of the Centre for Research on Globalization (CRG),

P.O. Box 55019, 11, rue Notre-Dame Ouest, Montréal, Québec, H2Y 4A7, Canada.

For more information, contact the publisher at the above address or by email at our website at www.globalresearch.ca.

The views expressed herein are the sole responsibility of the author and do not necessarily reflect those of the Centre for Research on Globalization. The publisher will not be held liable for the material contained in this book or any statements, omissions or inaccuracies pertaining thereto.

FIRST EDITION

Cover Photo © iStockphoto.com/peeterv

Cover graphics by Maja Romano © Global Research, 2012

Page layout and book design by Réjean Mc Kinnon

Printed and bound in Canada.
Printed on chlorine-free 100% post-consumer recycled canadian paper.

ISBN 978-0-9737147-5-3

Library and Archives Canada Cataloguing in Publication

Chossudovsky, Michel
Towards a World War III scenario :
the dangers of nuclear war / Michel Chossudovsky.

Includes bibliographical references.
ISBN 978-0-9737147-5-3

1. Nuclear warfare. 2. Nuclear warfare--Forecasting. 3. Nuclear weapons.
4. United States--Military policy--21st century. 5. World politics--2005-2015.
I. Title.

U263.C56 2012   355.02'17   C2012-900698-X

This book is dedicated to the memory of Dr. Alice C. Tang, who devoted her life to global peace, the pursuance of truth, military disarmament and the prevention of nuclear war.

Alice Tang's proposal was titled "Two Percent, No First Strike." The pledge would be that no nation shall spend more than 2 percent of its GDP on military purposes, and no nation would be a "first strike" aggressor with nuclear weapons.

Titles by Global Research Publishers

Michel Chossudovsky, *The Globalization of Poverty and the New World Order*, 2003.

Michel Chossudovsky, *America's "War on Terrorism"*, 2005.

F. William Engdahl, *Seeds of Destruction: The Hidden Agenda of Genetic Manipulation*, 2007.

Michel Chossudovsky and Andrew Gavin Marshall (Editors), *The Global Economic Crisis, The Great Depression of the XXI Century*, 2010.

TABLE OF CONTENTS

CHAPTER VI
REVERSING THE TIDE OF WAR

PREFACE

The World is at a critical crossroads. The Fukushima disaster in Japan has brought to the forefront the dangers of Worldwide nuclear radiation.

Coinciding with the onset of the nuclear crisis in Japan, a new regional war theater opened up in North Africa, under the disguise of a UN sponsored "humanitarian operation" with the mandate to "protect civilian lives".

These two seemingly unrelated events are of crucial importance in understanding both the nuclear issue as well as the ongoing US-NATO sponsored war, which has extended its grip into Libya.

The crisis in Japan has been described as "a nuclear war without a war". Its potential repercussions, which are yet to be fully assessed, are far more serious than the Chernobyl disaster, as acknowledged by several scientists.

The crisis in Japan has also brought into the open the unspoken relationship between nuclear energy and nuclear war. Nuclear energy is not a civilian economic activity. It is an appendage of the nuclear weapons industry which is controlled by the so-called defense contractors.

The powerful corporate interests behind nuclear energy and nuclear weapons overlap. In Japan at the height of the disaster, "the nuclear industry and government agencies [were] scrambling to prevent the discovery of atomic-bomb research facilities hidden inside Japan's civilian nuclear power plants".[1]

The media consensus is that the crisis at Fukushima's nuclear power plants has been contained.

The realities are otherwise. The Japanese government has been obliged to acknowledge that "the severity rating of its nuclear crisis ... matches that of the 1986 Chernobyl disaster". Moreover, the dumping of highly radioactive water into the Pacific Ocean constitutes a potential trigger to a process of global radioactive contamination.

Radioactive elements have not only been detected in the food chain in Japan, radioactive rain water has been recorded in California:

Hazardous radioactive elements being released in the sea and air around Fukushima accumulate at each step of various food chains (for example, into algae, crustaceans, small fish, bigger fish, then humans; or soil, grass, cow's meat and milk, then humans). Entering the body, these elements - called internal emitters - migrate to specific organs such as the thyroid, liver, bone, and brain, continuously irradiating small volumes of cells with high doses of alpha, beta and/or gamma radiation, and over many years often induce cancer.[2]

A New War Theater in North Africa

The War on Libya was launched within days of the Fukushima disaster. It was an integral part of the broader military agenda in the Middle East and Central Asia which until recently consisted of three distinct areas of conflict : Afghanistan and Pakistan (the AfPak War), Iraq, Palestine.

A fourth war theater has opened up in North Africa, which raises the issue of escalation over a vast geographical area.

These four war theaters are interrelated. They are part of a broader region of conflict, which extends from North Africa and the Middle East, engulfing a large part of the Mediterranean basin, to China's Western frontier with Afghanistan, and Northern Pakistan.

How does the war on Libya relate to this broader US-NATO military agenda?

Is a World War III scenario unfolding?

Is the use of nuclear weapons contemplated in North Africa?

With regard to nuclear doctrine, the concept of a US sponsored pre-emptive nuclear attack applies to a number of countries or "rogue states" including Libya.

An all-out war against the Qadhafi regime has been on the drawing board of the Pentagon for more than twenty years, Moreover, Libya was the first country to be tagged for a pre-emptive attack using tactical nuclear weapons.[3] The Clinton administration's plan to nuke Libya had been announced in no uncertain terms in a 1996 Department of Defense press briefing:

[The] Air Force would use the B61-11 [nuclear weapon] against Libya's alleged underground chemical weapons plant at Tarhunah if the President decided that the plant had to be destroyed. 'We could not take [Tarhunah] out of commission using strictly conventional weapons,' Smith told the Associated Press. *The B61-11 'would be the nuclear weapon of choice,'* he [Assistant Secretary of Defense Harold P. Smith] told *Jane's Defense Weekly*.[4]

Clinton's Defense Secretary William Perry had confirmed in a statement to the Senate Foreign Relations Committee that "the U.S. retained the option of using nuclear weapons against countries [e.g. Libya] armed with chemical and biological weapons."[5]

The Department of Defense's objective was to fast track the "testing" of the B61-11 nuclear bomb on an actual country and that country was Libya: "Even before the B61 came on line, Libya was identified as a potential target".[6]

While the 1996 plan to bomb Libya using tactical nuclear weapons was subsequently shelved, Libya was not removed from the "black list": "The Qadhafi regime" was therefore a target country for a pre-emptive ("defensive") nuclear attack. As revealed by William Arkin in early 2002:

The Bush administration, in a secret policy review... [had] ordered the Pentagon to draft contingency plans for the use of nuclear weapons against at least seven countries, *naming not only Russia and the "axis of evil" Iraq, Iran, and North Korea but also China, Libya and Syria.*[7]

Operation Odyssey Dawn. Nuclear Weapons against Libya? How Real is the Threat?

Has the project to nuke Libya been definitively shelved or was Libya still being contemplated as a potential target for a nuclear attack? (This preface serves as an update on the potential dangers of a nuclear war against a defenseless non-nuclear state).

The air campaign directed against Libya commenced on March 19, 2011. America deployed its Bat-shaped B-2 Spirit Stealth bombers operating out of the Whiteman Air Force Base in Missouri.

Described as "deadly and effective", the B-2 was used as an instrument of "humanitarian warfare".

Barely two weeks after the commencement of the war, the Pentagon announced the testing of the B61-11 nuclear bomb using the same B-2 Stealth bombers which had been deployed to Libya at the very outset of Operation Odyssey Dawn.

The B-2 Spirit Stealth bomber is the US Air Force's chosen "carrier" for the delivery of the B61-11 nuclear bomb. These timely tests pertained to the installed equipment, functionality and weapon's components of the B61-11 nuclear bomb. The tests were conducted by the B-2 bombers operating out of the same Air Force base, from which the B-2 bombing raid on Libya were conducted.[8]

Is the timing of these tests in any way related to the chronology of the Libya bombing campaign?

The U.S. Air Force Global Strike Command was in charge of both the JTA tests of the B61-11 as well as the deployment of three B-2 Spirit Stealth bombers to Libya on March 19 under operation Odyssey Dawn.

Both the deployment of the B-2s to the Libya war theater as well as the tests of the equipment of the B61-11 (using the B-2 bomber for delivery) were coordinated out of Whiteman Air Force base.

America's Long War: The Global Military Agenda

The US has embarked on a military adventure, "a long war", which threatens the future of humanity. The first two chapters of this book focus on the "Cult of Death and Destruction" underlying this global military agenda.

US-NATO weapons of mass destruction are portrayed as instruments of peace. Mini-nukes are said to be "harmless to the surrounding civilian population". Pre-emptive nuclear war is portrayed as a "humanitarian undertaking".

Nuclear war has become a multibillion dollar undertaking, which fills the pockets of US defense contractors. What is at stake is the outright "privatization of nuclear war".

US nuclear doctrine is intimately related to "America's War on Terrorism" and the alleged threat of Al Qaeda, which in a bitter irony is considered as an upcoming nuclear power.

Under the Obama administration, Islamic terrorists are said to be preparing to attack US cities. Proliferation is tacitly equated with "nuclear terrorism". Obama's nuclear doctrine puts particular emphasis on "nuclear terrorism" and on the alleged plans by Al Qaeda to develop and use nuclear weapons.

Chapter III focuses on America's Holy Crusade and the Battle for Oil. The "Global War on Terrorism" requires going after the terrorists, using advanced weapons systems. US foreign policy upholds a pre-emptive religious-like crusade against evil, which serves to obscure the real objectives of military action. In the inner consciousness of Americans, the attacks of September 11, 2001 justify acts of war and conquest against evil-doers.

The Global War on Terrorism is presented as a "clash of civilizations", a war between competing values and religions, when in reality it is an outright war of conquest, guided by strategic and economic objectives.

The lies behind 9/11 are known and documented. The American people's acceptance of this crusade against evil is not based on any rational understanding or analysis of the facts.

"The American inquisition" purports to extend Washington's sphere of influence. Military intervention is justified as part of an international campaign against "Islamic terrorists". Its ultimate intention, which is never mentioned in press reports, is territorial conquest and control over strategic resources. Ironically, under the Global War on Terrorism, these plans of conquest are instrumented by covertly supporting Islamic paramilitary armies, which are then used to destabilize non-compliant governments and impose Western standards of "governance" and "democracy".

World War III Scenario

The contours of a World War III scenario are discussed in Chapter IV. The Pentagon's global military design is one of world conquest.

The military deployment of US-NATO forces is occurring in several regions of the world simultaneously. Militarization at the global level is instrumented through the US military's Unified Command structure: the entire planet is divided up into geographic Combatant Commands under the control of the Pentagon.

According to (former) NATO Commander General Wesley Clark, the Pentagon's military road-map consists of a sequence of war theaters: "*[The] five-year campaign plan [includes]... a total of seven countries, beginning with Iraq, then Syria, Lebanon, Libya, Iran, Somalia and Sudan.*"

Chapter V focuses on war preparations pertaining to Iran, including the launching of a pre-emptive nuclear attack on the Islamic Republic.

While Iran remains on the Pentagon's drawing board, a fundamental shift in the sequencing of military operations has occurred.

The US-NATO-Israel alliance realizes that Iran has significant capabilities to respond and retaliate. With the onset of the US-NATO led war in North Africa, Washington and its allies have chosen to wage war on countries with lesser military capabilities. This factor in itself has been crucial in the decision by the US and its allies to put "the Iran operation" on hold, while launching a "humanitarian war" on Libya.

How to Reverse the Tide of War

Chapter VI focuses on antiwar actions directed against this diabolical military agenda.

Central to an understanding of war, is the media campaign which grants it legitimacy in the eyes of public opinion. A good versus evil dichotomy prevails. The perpetrators of war are presented as the victims. Public opinion is misled: "We must fight against evil in all its forms as a means to preserving the Western way of life."

Breaking the "big lie", which upholds war as a humanitarian undertaking, means breaking a criminal project of global destruction, in which the quest for profit is the overriding force. This profit-driven military agenda destroys human values and transforms people into unconscious zombies.

The holding of mass demonstrations and antiwar protests is not enough. What is required is the development of a broad and well organized grassroots antiwar network, across the land, nationally and internationally, which challenges the structures of power and authority.

People must mobilize not only against the military agenda, the authority of the state and its officials must also be challenged.

This war can be prevented if people forcefully confront their governments, pressure their elected representatives, organize at the local level in towns, villages and municipalities, spread the word, inform their fellow citizens as to the implications of a nuclear war, initiate debate and discussion within the armed forces.

The object of this book is to forcefully reverse the tide of war, challenge the war criminals in high office and the powerful corporate lobby groups which support them.

Break the American Inquisition.

Undermine the US-NATO-Israel military crusade.

Close down the weapons factories and the military bases.

Members of the armed forces should disobey orders and refuse to participate in a criminal war. Bring home the troops.

Acknowledgments

Research for this book was conducted over a period of almost ten years. Our sincere thanks to Global Research members and our readers, whose support has enabled us to develop our publishing and educational outreach activities.

I am much indebted to Maja Romano of the Centre for Research on Globalization (CRG) for her support in the editing process as well for the creative design of the front page graphics. I extend my thanks and appreciation to Réjean Mc Kinnon, for the careful typesetting, layout and production of the book and to Drew McKevitt and Finian Cunningham for their assistance in the copyediting of the manuscript.

NOTE:

The above preface was first drafted in May 2011 in relation to the publication of the E-book edition.

Michel Chossudovsky is an award-winning author, Professor of Economics (Emeritus) at the University of Ottawa. He is the Founder and Director of the Centre for Research on Globalization (CRG), Montreal and Editor of the globalresearch.ca website.
He is the author of The Globalization of Poverty and The New World Order (2003) and America's "War on Terrorism" (2005). He is also a contributor to the Encyclopaedia Britannica. His writings have been published in more than twenty languages.

NOTES

1. Yoichi Shimatsu, "Secret Weapons Program Inside Fukushima Nuclear Plant?", *Global Research,* http://globalresearch.ca/index.php?context=va&aid=24275, 12 April 2011.

2. Helen Caldicott, "Fukushima: Nuclear Apologists Play Shoot the Messenger on Radiation", *Global Research,* http://www.globalresearch.ca/index.php?context=va&aid= 24563, 30 April 2011.

3. Michel Chossudovsky, "America's Planned Nuclear Attack on Libya", *Global Research,* http://globalresearch.ca/index.php?context=va&aid=24049, 25 March 2011.

4. Federation of American Scientists, "The Birth of a Nuclear Bomb: B61-1", The Nuclear Information Project, http://www.nukestrat.com/us/afn/B61-11.htm, 14 July 2005.

5. *Ibid.,* see also Greg Mello, "The Birth Of a New Bomb", *The Washington Post,* http://www.oocities.org/marksrealm/project020.html, 1 June 1997.

6. Bulletin of the Atomic Scientists, September/October 1997, p. 27. For further details see Michel Chossudovsky, "America's Planned Nuclear Attack on Libya", *Global Research,* http://globalresearch.ca/index.php?context=va&aid=24049, 25 March 2011.

7. William Arkin, "Thinking the Unthinkable", *Los Angeles Times,* March 9, 2002.

8. In late March or early April 2011 (prior to April 4), the B-2 Spirit Stealth bomber from the 509th Bomber Wing, operating out of Whiteman Air Force Base, was used in the so-called "Joint Test Assembly" (JTA) of the B61 Mod 11 nuclear bomb. The announcement of these tests was made public on April 4; the precise date of the tests was not revealed, but one can reasonably assume that it was in the days prior to the April 4 press release by the National Nuclear Security Administration (NNSA), "NNSA Conducts Successful B61-11 JTA Flight Test", http://nnsa.energy.gov/mediaroom/pressreleases/ b61jta4411, 4 April 2011. For further details see Michel Chossudovsky, "Dangerous Crossroads: Is America Considering the Use of Nuclear Weapons against Libya?", *Global Research,* http://www.globalresearch.ca/index.php?context=va&aid=24202, 7 April 2011.

CHAPTER I
INTRODUCTION

Throughout the history of mankind there have been murderers and tyrants; and while it may seem momentarily that they have the upper hand, they have always fallen. (Mahatma Gandhi)

The United States has discarded pretensions to international legality and decency, and embarked on a course of raw imperialism run amok. (William Rockler, Nuremberg Tribunal prosecutor)

Those who can make you believe absurdities can make you commit atrocities. (François-Marie Arouet – *Voltaire*, 1694-1778)

The US and its NATO allies are preparing to launch a nuclear war directed against both Iran and North Korea with devastating consequences. This military adventure in the real sense of the word threatens the future of humanity. While one can conceptualize the loss of life and destruction resulting from present-day wars including Iraq and Afghanistan, it is impossible to fully comprehend the devastation which might result from a Third World War, using "new technologies" and advanced weapons, until it occurs and becomes a reality. The international community has endorsed nuclear war in the name of world peace. "Making the world safer" is the justification for launching a military operation which could potentially result in a nuclear holocaust.

But nuclear holocausts are not front page news! In the words of Mordechai Vanunu:

> The Israeli government is preparing to use nuclear weapons in its next war with the Islamic world. Here where I live, people often talk of the Holocaust. But each and every nuclear bomb is a Holocaust in itself. It can kill, devastate cities, destroy entire peoples.[1]

Realities are turned upside down. In a twisted logic, a "humanitarian war" using tactical nuclear weapons, which according to "expert scientific opinion" are "harmless to the surrounding civilian population", is upheld as a means to protecting the Western world from a nuclear attack.

The Cult of Killing and Destruction

The global killing machine is also sustained by an imbedded cult of killing and destruction which pervades Hollywood movies, not to mention the primetime war and crime TV series on network television. This cult of killing is endorsed by the CIA and the Pentagon which also support (finance) Hollywood productions as an instrument of war propaganda:

> Ex-CIA agent Bob Baer told us, "There's a symbiosis between the CIA and Hollywood" and revealed that former CIA director George Tenet is currently, "out in Hollywood, talking to studios."[2]

The killing machine is deployed at a global level, within the framework of the unified combat command structure. It is routinely upheld by the institutions of government, the corporate media, the mandarins and intellectuals of the New World Order in Washington's think tanks and strategic studies research institutes, as an unquestioned instrument of peace and global prosperity.

A culture of killing and violence has become imbedded in human consciousness. War is broadly accepted as part of a societal process: the Homeland needs to be "defended" and protected. "Legitimized violence" and extrajudicial killings directed against "terrorists" are upheld in western democracies, as necessary instruments of national security. A "humanitarian war" is upheld by the so-called international community. It is not condemned as a criminal act. Its main architects are rewarded for their contributions to world peace.

America's Mini-nukes

With regard to Iran, what is unfolding is the outright legitimization of war in the name of an illusive notion of global security. America's mini-nukes, with an explosive capacity of up to six times a Hiroshima bomb, are upheld as a humanitarian bomb, whereas Iran's nonexistent nuclear weapons are branded as an indisputable threat to global security.

When a US-sponsored nuclear war becomes an "instrument of peace", condoned and accepted by the world's institutions and the highest authority, including the United Nations, there is no turning back: human society has indelibly been precipitated headlong onto the path of self-destruction.

We are at a dangerous crossroads: the rules and guidelines governing the use of nuclear weapons have been "liberalized" (i.e. "deregulated" in relation to those prevailing during the Cold War era). The new doctrine states that Command, Control and Coordination (CCC) regarding the use of nuclear weapons should be "flexible", allowing geographic combat commanders to decide if and when to use nuclear weapons:

> Geographic combat commanders would be in charge of Theater Nuclear Operations (TNO), with a mandate not only to implement but also to formulate command decisions pertaining to nuclear weapons.[3]

We have reached a critical turning point in our history. It is absolutely essential that people across the land, nationally and internationally, understand the gravity of the present situation and act forcefully against their governments to reverse the tide of war.

The details of ongoing war preparations in relation to Iran and North Korea have been withheld from the public eye and the media is involved in acts of camouflage. The devastating impacts of a nuclear war are either trivialized or not mentioned. Instead, fake "crises" – e.g. a worldwide flu pandemic, a "false flag" nuclear attack by "Islamic terrorists" – are fabricated by the media, the governments, the intelligence apparatus and the Washington think tanks. While the real danger of nuclear war is barely acknowledged, these fake crises are invariably front page news.

A Third World War is no longer a hypothetical scenario. Already in 2007, President Bush hinted in no uncertain terms that if Iran did not comply with US demands, the US-NATO military might "reluctantly" be forced into in a World War III situation:

> We got a leader in Iran who has announced that he wants to destroy Israel. So I've told people that if you're interested in avoiding World War III, it seems like you ought to be interested in preventing them from have the knowledge necessary to make a nuclear weapon. I take the threat of Iran with a nuclear weapon very seriously... (George W. Bush, 17 October 2007)

War and the Economic Crisis

The broader implications of a US-NATO-Israel attack on Iran are far-reaching. The war and the economic crisis are intimately related. The war economy is financed by Wall Street, which stands as the creditor of the US administration. The US weapons producers are the recipients of the US Department of Defense's multibillion dollar procurement contracts for advanced weapons systems. In turn, "the battle for oil" in the Middle East and Central Asia directly serves the interests of the Anglo-American oil giants.

The US and its allies are beating the drums of war at the height of a worldwide economic depression, not to mention the most serious environmental catastrophe in world history. In a bitter twist, one of the major players (BP) on the Middle East Central Asia geopolitical chessboard, formerly known as the Anglo-Persian Oil Company, is the instigator of the ecological disaster in the Gulf of Mexico.

Real versus Fake Crises

In an utterly twisted logic, World War III is presented as a means to preserving world peace.

Iran is blamed for refusing to abide by the "reasonable demands" of "the international community".

Realities are twisted and turned upside down and Iran is being accused of wanting to start World War III. Inherent in US military doctrine, the victims of war are often heralded as the aggressor.

World War III is upheld as a *bona fide* humanitarian undertaking which contributes to global security. In a bitter irony, those who decide on the use of nuclear weapons believe their own propaganda. President and Commander in Chief Barack Obama believes his own lies.

Neither the war nor the worldwide economic depression are understood as part of an unprecedented crisis in world history. Ironically, the dangers to humanity of an all-out nuclear war do not instill fear and public concern.

An understanding of fundamental social and political events is replaced by a world of sheer fantasy, where "evil folks" are lurking. The purpose of these "fake crises" is to obfuscate the real crisis as well as instill fear and insecurity among the population:

> *The whole aim of practical politics is to keep the populace alarmed ... by menacing it with an endless series of hobgoblins, all of them imaginary... The urge to save humanity is almost always only a false face for the urge to rule it.*[4]

NOTES

1. See interview with Mordechai Vanunu, *Global Research,* http://www.globalre search.ca/index.php?context=viewArticle&code=20060102&articleId=1703, December 2005.

2. Matthew Alford and Robbie Graham, "Lights, Camera, Covert Action: The Deep Politics of Hollywood", *Global Research,* http://www.globalresearch.ca/index.php?con text=va&aid=11921, 31 January 2009.

3. Joint Chiefs of Staff, "Doctrine for Joint Nuclear Operations", Joint Publication 3-12, Washington DC, http://zfacts.com/metaPage/lib/zFacts_2005_03_15_Joint_Nu clear_Operations.pdf, March 2005.

4. Henri Louis Mencken, *In Defense of Women,* Dover Publications, 1918.

CHAPTER II
THE DANGERS OF
——— NUCLEAR WAR ———

*We have discovered the most terrible bomb in the history
of the world. It may be the fire destruction prophesied in
the Euphrates Valley Era, after Noah and his fabulous
Ark... This weapon is to be used against Japan... [We]
will use it so that military objectives and soldiers and
sailors are the target and not women and children. Even
if the Japs are savages, ruthless, merciless and fanatic,
we as the leader of the world for the common welfare
cannot drop that terrible bomb on the old capital or the
new... The target will be a purely military one... It seems
to be the most terrible thing ever discovered, but it can
be made the most useful.* (President Harry S. Truman,
Diary, July 25, 1945)

*The world will note that the first atomic bomb was
dropped on Hiroshima, a military base. That was because we wished in this first attack to avoid, insofar as
possible, the killing of civilians...* (President Harry S.
Truman in a radio speech to the Nation, August 9, 1945)

[Note: the first atomic bomb was dropped on Hiroshima
on August 6, 1945; the Second on Nagasaki, on August
9, on the same day as Truman's radio speech to the Na-
tion]

*Except for fools and madmen, everyone knows that nu-
clear war would be an unprecedented human catastrophe. A more or less typical strategic warhead has a yield
of 2 megatons, the explosive equivalent of 2 million tons
of TNT.*

*In a 2-megaton explosion over a fairly large city, build-
ings would be vaporized, people reduced to atoms and
shadows, outlying structures blown down like match-*

sticks and raging fires ignited. And if the bomb were exploded on the ground, an enormous crater, like those that can be seen through a telescope on the surface of the Moon, would be all that remained where midtown once had been. (Carl Sagan, *Nuclear Winter,* 1983, p. 14)

Any country that at present may be considering the nuclear option must acknowledge that by adopting such a decision, it would be endangering not only its own population but the entire world. It is time for the world to once again reflect upon the dangers of nuclear weapons, and this time follow the path to peace and eliminate the possibility of a global climate catastrophe [Nuclear Winter] induced by nuclear energy, for the first time since mid-last century...

The use of nuclear weapons in the event of a total attack against an enemy would be a suicidal action due to anomalous cold and darkness caused by the smoke from the fires generated by the bomb. In fact, it has been evidenced that the more nuclear weapons a country possesses, the less secure it is. (Dr. Alan Rock, September 2010)

Today there is an imminent risk of war with the use of that kind of weapon and I do not harbor the least doubt that an attack by the United States and Israel against the Islamic Republic of Iran would inevitably evolve towards a global nuclear conflict.

Albert Einstein himself stated unmistakably: "I do not know with what weapons World War III will be fought, but World War IV will be fought with sticks and stones". We fully comprehend what he wanted to convey, and he was absolutely right, yet in the wake of a global nuclear war, there wouldn't be anybody around to make use of those sticks and stones.

There would be "collateral damage", as the American political and military leaders always affirm, to justify the deaths of innocent people.

In a nuclear war the "collateral damage" would be the life of all humanity.

Let us have the courage to proclaim that all nuclear or conventional weapons, everything that is used to make war, must disappear! (Fidel Castro, October 15, 2010)

At no point since the first atomic bomb was dropped on Hiroshima on August 6th, 1945, has humanity been closer to the unthinkable – a nuclear holocaust which could potentially spread in terms of radioactive fallout over a large part of the Middle East.

All the safeguards of the Cold War era, which categorized the nuclear bomb as "a weapon of last resort", have been scrapped. "Offensive" military actions using nuclear warheads are now described as acts of "self-defense".

> The casualties from the direct effects of blast, radioactivity, and fires resulting from the massive use of nuclear weapons by the superpowers [of the Cold War era] would be so catastrophic that we avoided such a tragedy for the first four decades after the invention of nuclear weapons.[1]

During the Cold War, the doctrine of Mutually Assured Destruction (MAD) prevailed, namely that the use of nuclear weapons against the Soviet Union would result in "the destruction of both the attacker and the defender". In the post-Cold war era, US nuclear doctrine was redefined. The dangers of nuclear weapons have been obfuscated. Tactical weapons have been upheld as distinct, in terms of their impact, from the strategic thermonuclear bombs of the Cold War era. Tactical nuclear weapons are identical to the strategic nuclear bombs. The only things that differentiates these two categories of nuclear bombs are:

1) their delivery system;

2) their explosive yield (measured in mass of trinitrotoluene (TNT), in kilotons or megatons.

The tactical nuclear weapon or low yield mini-nuke is described as a small nuclear bomb, delivered in the same way as the earth-penetrating bunker buster bombs. Tactical nuclear weapons, in terms of in-theater delivery systems, are comparable to the bombs dropped on Hiroshima and Nagasaki in August 1945.

The Pentagon's *2001 Nuclear Posture Review* envisaged so-called "contingency plans" for an offensive "first strike use" of nuclear weapons, not only against "axis of evil" countries (including Iran and North Korea) but also against Russia and China.[2]

The adoption of the NPR by the US Congress in late 2002 provided a green light for carrying out the Pentagon's pre-emptive nuclear war doctrine, both in terms of military planning as well as defense procurement and production. Congress not only rolled back its prohibition on low yield nuclear weapons, it also provided funding "to pursue work on so-called mini-nukes". The financing was allocated to bunker buster (earth penetrator) tactical nuclear weapons as well as to the development of new nuclear weapons.[3]

Hiroshima Day 2003: Secret Meeting at Strategic Command Headquarters

On August 6, 2003, on Hiroshima Day, commemorating when the first atomic bomb was dropped on Hiroshima (August 6, 1945), a secret meeting was held behind closed doors at Strategic Command Headquarters at the Offutt Air Force Base in Nebraska. Senior executives from the nuclear industry and the military industrial complex were in attendance. This mingling of defense contractors, scientists and policy-makers was not intended to commemorate Hiroshima. The meeting was intended to set the stage for the development of a new generation of "smaller", "safer" and "more usable" nuclear weapons, to be used in the "in-theater nuclear wars" of the 21st Century.

In a cruel irony, the participants to this secret meeting, which excluded members of Congress, arrived on the anniversary of the Hiroshima bombing and departed on the anniversary of the attack on Nagasaki.

> More than 150 military contractors, scientists from the weapons labs, and other government officials gathered at the headquarters of the US Strategic Command in Omaha, Nebraska to plot and plan for the possibility of "full-scale nuclear

war", calling for the production of a new generation of nuclear weapons – more "usable" so-called "mini-nukes" and earth penetrating "bunker busters" armed with atomic warheads.[4]

According to a leaked draft of the agenda, the secret meeting included discussions on "mini-nukes" and "bunker-buster" bombs with nuclear war heads "for possible use against rogue states":

> We need to change our nuclear strategy from the Cold War to one that can deal with emerging threats... The meeting will give some thought to how we guarantee the efficacy of the (nuclear) stockpile.[5]

The Privatization of Nuclear War: US Military Contractors Set the Stage

The post-9/11 nuclear weapons doctrine was in the making, with America's major defense contractors directly involved in the decision-making process. The Hiroshima Day 2003 meetings had set the stage for the "privatization of nuclear war". Corporations not only reap multibillion-dollar profits from the production of nuclear bombs, they also have a direct voice in setting the agenda regarding the use and deployment of nuclear weapons. The nuclear weapons industry, which includes the production of nuclear devices as well as the missile delivery systems, etc., is controlled by a handful of defense contractors with Lockheed Martin, General Dynamics, Northrop Grunman, Raytheon and Boeing in the lead. It is worth noting that barely a week prior to the historic August 6, 2003 meeting, the National Nuclear Security Administration (NNSA) disbanded its advisory committee which provided an "independent oversight" on the US nuclear arsenal, including the testing and/or use of new nuclear devices.[6]

Meanwhile, the Pentagon had unleashed a major propaganda and public relations campaign with a view to upholding the use of nuclear weapons for the "defense of the American Homeland". In an utterly twisted logic, nuclear weapons were presented as a means to building peace and preventing "collateral damage". The Pentagon had intimated, in this regard, that the "mini-nukes" (with a yield of less than 5,000 tons) are harmless to civilians because the explosions "take place under ground". Each of these "mini-nukes", nonetheless, constitutes – in terms of explosion and potential radioactive fallout – between one-third and six times the atom bomb dropped on Hiroshima in 1945.

Vision 2030: Boosting the Production of "Hi-Tech Nuclear Weapons"

In 2005, a Department of Energy Task Force integrated by representatives of the defense industry was set to examine "The Nuclear Weapons Complex of the Future", a Vision 2030 of America's future nuclear arsenal.[7] The focus was on escalation with expanded levels of weapons production rather than the decommissioning of the Cold War arsenal. The Task Force recommended a major boost in the production of nuclear weapons through a process described as "Immediate Design of a Reliable Replacement Warhead (RRW)".[8]

The objective is to develop "the sustainable stockpile of the future" through the modernization of the existing stockpiles, namely through the refurbishing of the Cold War nuclear stockpile. Rather than decommissioning obsolete nuclear warheads, the Cold War nuclear arsenal is slated to be modernized, namely the nuclear materials will be used in the production of the modernized weapons systems. In this process, the number of nuclear warheads, estimated at more than 5000 will be reduced, with a "near-term lower limit of 1700 for Operationally Deployed Strategic Nuclear Weapons (ODSNW)."[9]

The Task Force recommended the development a new "family of modern nuclear weapons, designed with greater margin to meet military requirements while incorporating state-of-the-art surety requirements... This family of weapons will form the basis of the sustainable stockpile of the future that will replace the current Cold War stockpile."[10] The task force further recommended the creation of a Consolidated Nuclear Production Center (CNPC), namely, "the building [of] a modern set of production facilities with 21st century cutting-edge nuclear component production, manufacturing, and assembly technologies, all at one location...When operational, the CNPC will produce and dismantle all RRW weapons."[11]

The longer term objective is to create "The Agile and Responsive Nuclear Weapons Complex of 2030".

Formally endorsed by the US Congress in late 2003, the mini-nukes are considered to be "safe for civilians". Once this assumption was built into military planning, it constituted a consensus, which was no longer the object of critical debate. Decisions pertaining to the use of these nuclear weapons will be based on the prior "scientific" assessments underlying this consensus that they are "not dangerous for civilians". Based on this premise, the US Congress in 2003 granted the "green light" to the Pentagon and the military industrial complex to use tactical nuclear weapons in "conventional war theaters" (e.g. in the Middle East and Central Asia) alongside conventional weapons. In December 2003, the US Congress allocated 6.3 billion dollars solely for 2004, to develop this new generation of "defensive" nuclear weapons.

9/11 Military Doctrine: Nuclear Weapons and the "Global War on Terrorism"

To justify pre-emptive military actions, the National Security Doctrine requires the fabrication of a terrorist threat – i.e. "an outside enemy". It also needs to link these terrorist threats to "state sponsorship" by so-called "rogue states". Spelled out in the 2002 National Security Strategy (NSS), the pre-emptive defensive war doctrine and the "global war on terrorism" (GWOT) directed against Al Qaeda constitute essential building blocks of the Pentagon's propaganda campaign.

In the wake of September 11, 2001, US nuclear doctrine became integrated into the "war on terrorism". The objective was to present "pre-emptive military action" – meaning war as an act of "self-defense" – against two categories of enemies: "rogue states" and "Islamic terrorists", both of which are said to possess weapons of mass destruction:

> The war against terrorists of global reach is a global enterprise of uncertain duration... America will act against such emerging threats before they are fully formed...

> Rogue states and terrorists do not seek to attack us using conventional means. They know such attacks would fail. Instead, they rely on acts of terror and, potentially, the use of weapons of mass destruction...

The targets of these attacks are our military forces and our civilian population, in direct violation of one of the principal norms of the law of warfare. As was demonstrated by the losses on September 11, 2001, mass civilian casualties is the specific objective of terrorists and these losses would be exponentially more severe if terrorists acquired and used weapons of mass destruction.

The United States has long maintained the option of pre-emptive actions to counter a sufficient threat to our national security. The greater the threat, the greater is the risk of inaction – and the more compelling the case for taking anticipatory action to defend ourselves... To forestall or prevent such hostile acts by our adversaries, the United States will, if necessary, act pre-emptively.[12]

This "anticipatory action" under the NSS includes the use of tactical nuclear weapons, which are now classified as in theater weapons alongside conventional weapons. Nuclear weapons are presented as performing defensive functions to be used against so-called "rogue states" and terrorist organizations, including Al Qaeda.

The revised Doctrine for Joint Nuclear Operations (March 2005) envisaged five scenarios where the "use of nuclear weapons might be requested":

To counter an adversary intending to use weapons of mass destruction against U.S., multinational or allies forces or civilian populations;

To counter an imminent attack from an adversary's biological weapons that only effects from nuclear weapons can safely destroy;

To attack adversary installations including weapons of mass destruction, deep, hardened bunkers containing chemical or biological weapons, or the command and control infrastructure required for the adversary to execute a WMD attack against the United States or its friends and allies;

To counter potentially overwhelming adversary conventional forces;

To demonstrate U.S. intent and capability to use nuclear weapons to deter adversary WMD use.[13]

Al Qaeda: "Upcoming Nuclear Power"

The September 11, 2001 terrorist attacks served to galvanize public opinion, particularly in the US, in support of the pre-emptive war doctrine. The post-9/11 propaganda ploy emanating from the CIA and the Pentagon consists in presenting Al Qaeda as capable of developing a nuclear device. According to a report by the CIA's Intelligence Directorate (released two months prior to the August 2003 "Hiroshima Day" meeting in Nebraska), Al Qaeda has the ability of developing an "Improvised Nuclear Device" (IND):

> Al-Qa'ida and associated extremist groups have a wide variety of potential agents and delivery means to choose from for chemical, biological, radiological, or nuclear (CBRN) attacks.
>
> Al-Qa'ida's end goal is the use of CBRN to cause mass casualties...
>
> Usama Bin Ladin's operatives may try to launch conventional attacks against the nuclear industrial infrastructure of the United States in a bid to cause contamination, disruption, and terror. A document recovered from an al-Qa'ida facility in Afghanistan contained a sketch of a crude nuclear device...
>
> An Improvised Nuclear Device... is intended to cause a yield-producing nuclear explosion. An IND could consist of diverted nuclear weapon components, a modified nuclear weapon, or indigenous-designed device.
>
> INDs can be categorized into two types: implosion and gun assembled... INDs require fissile material – highly enriched uranium or plutonium – to produce nuclear yield.[14]

While the media has its eyes riveted on Islamic terrorists and Al Qaeda, the threats to global security resulting from Washington's pre-emptive nuclear doctrine are barely mentioned. There is only deafening silence: the August 6, 2003 "Hiroshima Day" meeting in Nebraska was not covered by the mainstream media.

In a 2006 testimony to the US Senate Budget Committee, Secretary of State Condoleezza Rice accused Iran and Syria of destabilizing the Middle East and providing support to militant Islamic groups. She described Iran as "a central banker for terrorism", notwithstanding the fact (amply documented) that Al Qaeda has been supported and financed from its inception in the early 1980s by none other than the CIA[15]:

> It's not just Iran's nuclear program but also their support for terrorism around the world. They are, in effect, the central banker for terrorism.[16]

Obama's Nuclear Doctrine: The 2010 Nuclear Posture Review

Under the Obama administration, terrorists are said to be working hand in glove with the Islamic Republic of Iran. Proliferation is tacitly equated with "nuclear terrorism". *The 2010 Nuclear Posture Review* puts particular emphasis on "nuclear terrorism" and on the alleged plans by Al Qaeda to develop and use nuclear weapons.[17]

> The threat of global nuclear war has become remote, but the risk of nuclear attack has increased. As President Obama has made clear, today's most immediate and extreme danger is nuclear terrorism. *Al Qaeda and their extremist allies are seeking nuclear weapons. We must assume they would use such weapons if they managed to obtain them.*
>
> The vulnerability to theft or seizure of vast stocks of such nuclear materials around the world, and the availability of sensitive equipment and technologies in the nuclear black market, create a serious risk that terrorists may acquire what they need to build a nuclear weapon. Today's other pressing threat is nuclear proliferation. Additional countries – especially those at odds with the United States, its allies and partners, and the broader international community – may acquire nuclear weapons. In pursuit of their nuclear ambitions, North Korea and Iran have violated non-proliferation obligations, defied directives of the United Nations Security Council, pursued missile delivery capabilities, and resisted international efforts to resolve through diplomatic means the crises they have created. Their provocative behavior has increased instability in their regions and could generate pressures in neighboring countries for considering nuclear deterrent options of their own. Continued non-compliance with non-proliferation norms by these and other countries would seriously weaken the Nuclear Non-

Proliferation Treaty (NPT), with adverse security implications for the United States and the international community.[18]

Under the banner of nuclear non-proliferation, the US Administration's objective is to gain a monopoly over the stocks as well as the production of nuclear materials worldwide. The latter activity is described as "securing nuclear materials", namely taking control of those nuclear materials:

> Unless today's dangerous trends are arrested and reversed, before very long we will be living in a world with a steadily growing number of nuclear-armed states and *an increasing likelihood of terrorists getting their hands on nuclear weapons.* The U.S. approach to preventing nuclear proliferation and nuclear terrorism includes three key elements.
>
> First, we seek to bolster the nuclear non-proliferation regime and its centerpiece, the *NPT, by reversing the nuclear ambitions of North Korea and Iran... impeding illicit nuclear trade.* Second, we are accelerating efforts to implement President Obama's initiative to secure all vulnerable nuclear materials worldwide in four years. And third, we are pursuing arms control efforts – including the New Strategic Arms Reduction Treaty (New START), ratification and entry into force of the Comprehensive Nuclear Test Ban Treaty, and negotiation of a verifiable Fissile Material Cutoff Treaty – as a means of strengthening our ability to mobilize broad international support for the measures needed to reinforce the non-proliferation regime and *secure nuclear materials worldwide.*[19]

Post-9/11 Nuclear Doctrine

In the post-9/11 era, the distinction between tactical nuclear weapons and the conventional battlefield arsenal becomes increasingly blurred. America's new nuclear doctrine is based on "a mix of strike capabilities". The latter, which specifically applies to the Pentagon's planned aerial bombing of Iran, envisages the use of nukes in combination with conventional weapons.

As in the case of the first atomic bomb, which in the words of President Harry Truman, "was dropped on Hiroshima, a military base", today's "mini-nukes" are heralded as "safe for the surrounding civilian population".

Known in official Washington, as "Joint Publication 3-12", the new *Doctrine for Joint Nuclear Operations* (DJNO) (March 2005) calls for "integrating conventional and nuclear attacks" under a unified and "integrated" Command and Control (C2).[20]

It largely describes war planning as a management decision-making process, where military and strategic objectives are to be achieved through a mix of instruments, with little concern for the resulting loss of human life.

Military planning focuses on "the most efficient use of force" – i.e. an optimal arrangement of different weapons systems to achieve stated military goals. In this context, nuclear and conventional weapons are considered to be "part of the tool box", from which military commanders can pick and choose the instruments that they require in accordance with "evolving circumstances" in the war theater. (None of these weapons in the Pentagon's "tool box", including conventional bunker buster bombs, cluster bombs, mini-nukes, chemical and biological weapons, are described as "weapons of mass destruction" when used by the United States of America and its coalition partners.)

The stated objective is to:

> Ensure *the most efficient use of force* and provide US leaders with a broader range of [nuclear and conventional] strike options to address immediate contingencies. Integration of conventional and nuclear forces is therefore crucial to the success of any comprehensive strategy. This integration will ensure optimal targeting, minimal collateral damage, and reduce the probability of escalation.[21]

The new nuclear doctrine turns concepts and realities upside down. It not only denies the devastating impacts of nuclear weapons, it states, in no uncertain terms, that nuclear weapons are "safe" and their use in the battlefield will ensure "minimal collateral damage and reduce the probability of escalation". The issue of radioactive fallout is not even acknowledged with regard to tactical nuclear weapons, neither is the issue of "Nuclear Winter". These various guiding principles which describe nukes as "safe for civilians" constitute a consensus within the military, which is then fed into the military manuals, providing relevant "green light" criteria to geographical commanders in the war theater.

"Defensive" and "Offensive" Actions

The post-911 nuclear doctrine as formulated in the *2001 Nuclear Posture Review* had set the stage for the pre-emptive use of nuclear weapons in the Middle East, specifically against Iran.[22]

The Doctrine for Joint Nuclear Operations goes one step further in blurring the distinction between "defensive" and "offensive" military actions:

> The new triad offers a mix of strategic *offensive and defensive capabilities* that includes *nuclear and non-nuclear strike capabilities, active and passive defenses*, and a robust research, development, and industrial infrastructure to *develop, build, and maintain offensive forces and defensive systems...*[23]

The new nuclear doctrine, however, goes beyond pre-emptive acts of "self-defense"; it calls for "anticipatory action" using nuclear weapons against a "rogue enemy" which allegedly plans to develop WMD at some undefined future date:

> Responsible security planning *requires preparation for threats that are possible, though perhaps unlikely today*. The lessons of military history remain clear: unpredictable, irrational conflicts occur. Military forces must prepare to counter weapons and capabilities that exist or will exist in the near term *even if no immediate likely scenarios for war are at hand*. To maximize deterrence of WMD use, *it is essential US forces prepare to use nuclear weapons effectively and that US forces are determined to employ nuclear weapons if necessary to prevent or retaliate against WMD use*.[24]

Nukes would serve to prevent a non-existent WMD program (e.g. Iran) prior to its development. This twisted formulation goes far beyond the premises of the 2001 Nuclear Posture Review and NPSD

17, which state that the US can retaliate with nuclear weapons if attacked with WMD:

> The United States will make clear that it reserves the right to respond with overwhelming force – including potentially nuclear weapons – to the use of [weapons of mass destruction] against the United States, our forces abroad, and friends and allies...[25]

"Integration" of Nuclear and Conventional Weapons Plans

The Doctrine for Joint Nuclear Operations outlines the procedures governing the use of nuclear weapons and the nature of the relationship between nuclear and conventional war operations. The DJNO states that the:

> Use of nuclear weapons within a [war] theater *requires that nuclear and conventional plans be integrated to the greatest extent possible.*[26]

The implications of this "integration" are far-reaching because once the decision is taken by the Commander in Chief, namely the President of the United States, to launch a joint conventional-nuclear military operation, there is a risk that tactical nuclear weapons could be used without requesting subsequent presidential approval. In this regard, execution procedures under the jurisdiction of the theater commanders pertaining to nuclear weapons are described as "flexible and allow for changes in the situation":

> *Geographic combatant commanders are responsible for defining theater objectives and developing nuclear plans* required to support those objectives, including selecting targets. When tasked, CDRUSSTRATCOM, as a supporting combatant commander, provides detailed planning support to meet theater planning requirements. All theater nuclear option planning follows prescribed Joint Operation Planning and Execution System procedures to formulate and implement an effective response within the timeframe permitted by the crisis...
>
> Since options do not exist for every scenario, combatant commanders must have a capability to perform crisis action plan-

ning and execute those plans. Crisis action planning provides the capability to develop new options, or modify existing options, when current limited or major response options are inappropriate...

Command, control, and coordination must be flexible enough to allow the geographic combatant commander to strike time-sensitive targets such as mobile missile launch platforms.[27]

Theater Nuclear Operations (TNO)

While presidential approval is formally required to launch a nuclear war, geographic combat commanders would be in charge of Theater Nuclear Operations (TNO), with a mandate not only to implement but also to formulate command decisions pertaining to nuclear weapons.[28] We are no longer dealing with "the risk" associated with "an accidental or inadvertent nuclear launch" as outlined by former Secretary of Defense Robert S. McNamara, but with a military decision-making process which provides military commanders, from the Commander in Chief down to the geographical commanders, with discretionary powers to use tactical nuclear weapons. Moreover, because these "smaller" tactical nuclear weapons have been reclassified by the Pentagon as "safe for the surrounding civilian population", thereby "minimizing the risk of collateral damage", there are no overriding built-in restrictions which prevent their use.[29]

Once a decision to launch a military operation is taken (e.g. aerial strikes on Iran), theater commanders have a degree of latitude. What this signifies in practice is once the presidential decision is taken, USSTRATCOM in liaison with theater commanders can decide on the targeting and type of weaponry to be used. Stockpiled tactical nuclear weapons are now considered to be an integral part of the battlefield arsenal. In other words, nukes have become "part of the tool box" used in conventional war theaters.

Planned Aerial Attacks on Iran

An operational plan to wage aerial attacks on Iran has been in "a state of readiness" since June 2005. Essential military hardware to wage this operation has been deployed.[30]

In 2005, Vice President Dick Cheney ordered USSTRATCOM to draft a "contingency plan", which included "a large-scale air assault on Iran employing both conventional and tactical nuclear weapons."[31]

What is diabolical in Cheney's contingency plan is that the justification to wage war on Iran rests on Iran's presumed involvement in a terrorist attack on America, "which has not yet occurred":

> The plan includes a large-scale air assault on Iran employing both conventional and tactical nuclear weapons. Within Iran there are more than 450 major strategic targets, including numerous suspected nuclear-weapons-program development sites. Many of the targets are hardened or are deep underground and could not be taken out by conventional weapons, hence the nuclear option. As in the case of Iraq, the response is not conditional on Iran actually being involved in the act of terrorism directed against the United States. Several senior Air Force officers involved in the planning are reportedly appalled at the implications of what they are doing – that Iran is being set up for an unprovoked nuclear attack – but no one is prepared to damage his career by posing any objections.[32]

Cheney's proposed "contingency plan" did not focus on preventing a Second 9/11. The Cheney plan was predicated on the presumption that Iran would be behind a Second 9/11 and that punitive bombings would immediately be activated, prior to conducting an investigation, much in the same way as the attacks on Afghanistan in October 2001, allegedly in retribution for the role of the Taliban government in support of the 9/11 terrorists:

> At a deeper level, it implies that "9/11-type terrorist attacks" are recognized in Cheney's office and the Pentagon as appropriate means of legitimizing wars of aggression against any country selected for that treatment by the regime and its corporate propaganda-amplification system.[33]

Are US military planners since the Bush administration waiting in limbo for a war pretext incident (e.g. a "Second 9/11") to launch a military operation directed against Iran?

Global Warfare: The Role of US Strategic Command (USSTRATCOM)

Global military operations are coordinated out of US Strategic Command Headquarters (USSTRATCOM) at the Offutt Air Force base in Nebraska, in liaison with the regional commands of the unified combatant commands (e.g. US Central Command in Florida, which is responsible for the Middle East-Central Asian region), as well as coalition command units in Israel, Turkey, the Persian Gulf and the Diego Garcia military base in the Indian Ocean. Military planning and decision making at a country level by individual allies of US-NATO as well as "partner nations" is integrated into a global military design including the weaponization of space. What this means is that the coordination of a large scale attack on Iran, including the various scenarios of escalation in and beyond the broader Middle East Central Asian region would be coordinated by USSTRATCOM.

Coinciding with Cheney's 2005 "Contingency Plan" to attack Iran, a significant shift in USSTRATCOM's mandate was implemented. USSTRATCOM was identified as "the lead Combatant Command for integration and synchronization of DoD-wide efforts in combating weapons of mass destruction." To implement this mandate, a brand new command unit entitled *Joint Functional Component Command Space and Global Strike,* or JFCCSGS, was created. Under its new mandate, USSTRATCOM has a responsibility for "overseeing a global strike plan" consisting of both conventional and nuclear weapons. In military jargon, it is slated to play the role of "a global integrator charged with the missions of Space Operations; Information Operations; Integrated Missile Defense; Global Command & Control; Intelligence, Surveillance and Reconnaissance; Global Strike; and Strategic Deterrence." USSTRATCOM's responsibilities include: "leading, planning, & executing strategic deterrence operations" at a global level, "synchronizing global missile defense plans and operations", "synchronizing regional combat plans", etc. USSTRATCOM is the lead agency in the coordination of modern warfare.

Overseen by USSTRATCOM, JFCCSGS would be responsible for the launching of military operations "using nuclear or conventional weapons" in compliance with the Bush administration's 2002 nuclear doctrine. Both categories of weapons would be integrated into a "joint strike operation" under unified Command and Control:

> The Defense Department is upgrading its nuclear strike plans to reflect new presidential guidance and a transition in war planning from the top-heavy Single Integrated Operational Plan of the Cold War to a family of smaller and more flexible strike plans designed to defeat today's adversaries. The new central strategic war plan is known as OPLAN (Operations Plan) 8044... This revised, detailed plan provides more flexible options to assure allies, and dissuade, deter, and if necessary, defeat adversaries in a wider range of contingencies...
>
> One member of the new family is CONPLAN 8022, a concept plan for the quick use of nuclear, conventional, or information warfare capabilities to destroy – preemptively, if necessary – "time-urgent targets" anywhere in the world. Defense Secretary Donald Rumsfeld issued an Alert Order in early 2004 that directed the military to put CONPLAN 8022 into effect. As a result, the Bush administration's preemption policy is now operational on long-range bombers, strategic submarines on deterrent patrol, and presumably intercontinental ballistic missiles (ICBMs).[34]

The operational implementation of the Global Strike Plan was initially under CONCEPT PLAN (CONPLAN) 8022, which consisted of "an actual plan that the Navy and the Air Force translate into a strike package for their submarines and bombers."[35] CONPLAN 8022 was "the overall umbrella plan for sort of the pre-planned strategic scenarios involving nuclear weapons... It specifically focused on these new types of threats – Iran, North Korea – proliferators and potentially terrorists too... There's nothing that says that they can't use CONPLAN 8022 in limited scenarios against Russian and Chinese targets."[36]

While the controversial CONPLAN 8022 was abandoned in 2008, the fundamental tenets of Global Strike and global warfare prevail. The *Joint Functional Component Command for Space and Global*

Strike (later changed to Joint Functional Component Command for Global Strike and Integration, JFCC GSI) remains functionally intact:

> The *Concept of Operations document* for the new command shows that its responsibilities reach far beyond Global Strike to all strategic strike planning for OPLAN 8044. Through JFCC GSI, STRATCOM is transforming its formerly secluded strategic nuclear strike enterprise into an integrated planning and strike service for national-level and regional combatant commanders.[37]

The JFCC is the cornerstone of global warfare, to "combat adversary weapons of mass destruction worldwide" based on "integrated strike capabilities":

Mission Statement

JFCC GS integrates all elements of military power in support of the Commander, United States Strategic Command (USSTRATCOM) global missions; synchronizes USSTRATCOM global deterrence capabilities and Department of Defense effects to combat adversary weapons of mass destruction worldwide; provides integrated global strike capabilities to deter and dissuade threats and when directed, defeat adversaries through decisive joint global kinetic and non-kinetic combat effects.

Background

JFCC GS originated in a directive issued by the Commander, USSTRATCOM in July 2006. The USSTRATCOM JFCCs were formed to further operationalize USSTRATCOM missions and allow the Headquarters, USSTRATCOM to focus on strategic-level integration and advocacy. JFCC GS is designed to optimize planning, execution and force management for the assigned missions of deterring attacks against the United States, its territories, possessions and bases.

JFCC GS plays a critical role in integrating USSTRATCOM global capabilities into theater operations. JFCC GS provides a unique ability to command and control global strike capabilities, as well as to build a plan rapidly to integrate all military capabilities and quickly bring them to bear on the battlefield.

- Maintains the nation's strategic deterrence (nuclear) war plan
- Maintains an environment to share information, integrate effects, and synchronize ongoing operations among mission partners
- Delivers deliberate/adaptive planning products for kinetic (nuclear and conventional) and non-kinetic capabilities
- Provides rapid Course Of Action (COA) development capabilities to optimize global strike operations
- Leads Global Strike planning to deliver timely effects against fleeting or high-value targets at global ranges
- Plans and coordinates global strike objectives for Joint and Combatant Command (COCOM) exercises, wargames and experiments
- Leads operational integration of USSTRATCOM Headquarters, JFCCs, other COCOM activities directed toward the goal of a seamless, constant integration of processes and products to help the warfighter discover and use actionable knowledge
- Provides operational control of two Cruise Missile Support Agencies (CMSA PAC in Hawaii and CMSA LANT in Virginia)[38]

Nuclear Weapons Deployment Authorization

The planning of the aerial bombings of Iran started in mid-2004, pursuant to the formulation of CONPLAN 8022 in early 2004. In May 2004, National Security Presidential Directive *NSPD 35 entitled Nuclear Weapons Deployment Authorization* was issued. The content of this highly sensitive document remains a carefully guarded state secret. There was no mention of NSPD 35 by the media nor even in Congressional debates. While its content remains classified, the presumption is that NSPD 35 pertains to the deployment of tactical nuclear weapons in the Middle East war theater in compliance with CONPLAN 8022.

Following the release of The Nuclear Weapons Deployment Authorization NSPD 35, a Turkish press report intimated that the US military had been "deploying B61-type tactical nuclear weapons in southern Iraq as part of a plan to hit Iran from this area if and when Iran responds to an Israeli attack on its nuclear facilities."[39] What the *Yeni Safak* report suggests is that conventional weapons would be used in the first instance, and if Iran were to retaliate in response to US-Israeli aerial attacks, tactical B61 nuclear weapons would be used. This retaliation using mini-nukes would be consistent with the guidelines contained in both the 2001 Nuclear Posture Review and NSPD 17.

Israel's Stockpiling of Conventional and Nuclear Weapons

Israel is part of the military alliance and is slated to play a major role in the planned attacks on Iran.[40] Confirmed by several press reports, Israel has taken delivery, starting in September 2004, of some 500 US-produced BLU 109 bunker buster bombs.[41] The first procurement order for BLU 109 [Bomb Live Unit] dates to September 2004. In April 2005, Washington confirmed that Israel was to take delivery of 100 of the more sophisticated bunker buster GBU-28 bomb produced by Lockheed Martin.[42] The GBU-28 is described as "a 5,000-pound laser-guided conventional munitions that uses a 4,400-pound penetrating warhead." It was used in the Iraqi war theater:

> The Pentagon [stated] that... the sale to Israel of 500 BLU-109 warheads [was] meant to contribute significantly to U.S. strategic and tactical objectives... Mounted on satellite-guided bombs, BLU-109s can be fired from F-15 or F-16 jets, U.S.-made aircraft in Israel's arsenal. This year Israel received the first of a fleet of 102 long-range F-16Is from Washington, its main ally. Israel very likely manufactures its own bunker busters, but they are not as robust as the 2,000-pound (910 kg) BLUs," Robert Hewson, editor of Jane's Air-Launched Weapons, told Reuters.[43]

The report does not confirm whether Israel has stockpiled and deployed the thermonuclear version of the bunker buster bomb. Nor does it indicate whether the Israeli made bunker buster bombs are equipped with nuclear warheads. It is worth noting that this stock-piling of bunker buster bombs by Israel followed shortly after the Release of the *NPSD 35, Nuclear Weapons Deployment Authorization* (May 2004).

Israel possesses 100-200 *strategic nuclear warheads*. In 2003, Washington and Tel Aviv confirmed that they were collaborating in "the deployment of US-supplied harpoon cruise missiles armed with nuclear warheads in Israel's fleet of Dolphin-class submarines."[44] In the context of the preparations of aerial strikes against Iran, Israel has taken delivery of two new German-produced submarines "that could launch nuclear-armed cruise missiles for a 'second-strike' deterrent."[45]

Israel's tactical nuclear weapons capabilities are not known. Israel's participation in the aerial attacks will also act as a political bombshell throughout the Middle East. It would contribute to escalation, with a war zone which could extend initially into Lebanon and Syria. The entire region from the Eastern Mediterranean to Central Asia and Afghanistan's Western frontier would be affected.

The Role of Western Europe

Several Western European countries, officially considered as "non-nuclear states", possess US Made tactical nuclear weapons, supplied to them by the Pentagon. The US has supplied some 480 B61 thermonuclear bombs to five non-nuclear NATO countries including Belgium, Germany, Italy, the Netherlands and Turkey, and one nuclear country, the United Kingdom. Casually disregarded by the Vienna-based UN Nuclear Watch, the US has actively contributed to the proliferation of nuclear weapons in Western Europe.

As part of this European stockpiling, Turkey, which is a partner of the US-led coalition against Iran along with Israel, possesses some 90 thermonuclear B61 bunker buster bombs at the Incirlik nuclear air base.[46]

Recent (unconfirmed) reports suggest that the number of tactical nuclear weapons deployed in Western Europe may have been reduced to 200-250. While some of these tactical nuclear weapons have been decommissioned, part of the stockpile may have been transferred from Western Europe to military bases in the Middle East and Central Asia as part of the Nuclear Weapons Deployment Authorization (NSPD 35) (discussed above).

NATO considers this arsenal as belonging to the conventional battlefield:

> The bombs are considered tactical or battlefield nukes – as opposed to strategic or long-range nuclear weapons – because they are designed to be dropped on attacking armies, not the cities, infrastructure or industry targeted by strategic missiles and bombs.[47]

The tactical nuclear weapon is described as a defensive rather than offensive weapon. In a twisted logic, NATO's nuclear deployment of tactical nuclear weapons is intended to support the Alliance's doctrine of collective security.

Consistent with US and NATO nuclear policy, the stockpiling and deployment of B61 in Western Europe are intended for targets in the Middle East. Moreover, in accordance with "NATO strike plans", these thermonuclear B61 bunker buster bombs (stockpiled by the "non-nuclear states") could be launched "against targets in Russia or countries in the Middle East such as Syria and Iran."[48]

Moreover, confirmed by (partially) declassified documents, released under the U.S. Freedom of Information Act:

> Arrangements were made in the mid-1990s to allow the use of U.S. nuclear forces in Europe outside the area of responsibility of U.S. European Command (EUCOM). As a result of these arrangements, *EUCOM now supports CENTCOM nuclear missions in the Middle East, including, potentially, against Iran and Syria.*[49]

With the exception of the US, no other nuclear power "has nuclear weapons earmarked for delivery by non-nuclear countries."[50] While these "non-nuclear states" casually accuse Tehran of developing nuclear weapons, without documentary evidence, their B61 tactical nukes, under national command, are targeted at Iran: a clear case of "double standards" by the IAEA and the "international community".

Germany: *De Facto* Nuclear Power

Among the five "non-nuclear states", sources indicate that "Germany remains the most heavily nuclearized country with three nuclear bases (two of which are fully operational) and may store as many as 150 [B61 bunker buster] bombs."[51] In accordance with "NATO strike plans" (mentioned above), these tactical nuclear weapons are also targeted at the Middle East. While Germany is not officially a nuclear power, it produces nuclear warheads for the French Navy. It stockpiles nuclear warheads and it has the capabilities of delivering nuclear weapons. *The European Aeronautic Defense and Space Company - EADS,* a Franco-German-Spanish joint venture, controlled by Deutsche Aerospace and the powerful Daimler Group, is Europe's second largest military producer, supplying France's M51 nuclear missile.

Pre-emptive Nuclear War: NATO's 2010 Strategic Concept

NATO's Strategic Concept, adopted in November 2010 endorses, on behalf of all NATO members, the pre-emptive nuclear war doctrine as an instrument of peace. NATO's stated objective is to "maintain an appropriate mix of nuclear and conventional forces" as well as "ensure the broadest possible participation of Allies in collective defence planning on nuclear roles, in peacetime basing of nuclear forces, and in command, control and consultation arrangements."[52]

> Deterrence, based on an appropriate mix of nuclear and conventional capabilities, remains a core element of our overall strategy... The supreme guarantee of the security of the Allies is provided by the strategic nuclear forces of the Alliance, particularly those of the United States; the independent strategic nuclear forces of the United Kingdom and France, which have a deterrent role of their own, contribute to the overall deterrence and security of the Allies.[53]

These 2010 provisions are in marked contrast to NATO's 1999 Strategic Concept which advocated the notion that "NATO's nuclear forces [would] no longer target any country."[54]

The World is at a Critical Crossroads

It is not Iran and North Korea which are a threat to global security but the United States of America and Israel. In recent developments, Western European governments – including the so-called "non-nuclear states" which possess nuclear weapons – have joined the bandwagon. In chorus, Western Europe and the member states of the Atlantic alliance (NATO) have endorsed the US-led military initiative against Iran.

The Pentagon's planned aerial attacks on Iran involve scenarios using both nuclear and conventional weapons. While this does not imply the use of nuclear weapons, the potential danger of a Middle East nuclear holocaust must nonetheless be taken seriously. It must become a focal point of the antiwar movement, particularly in the United States, Western Europe, Israel and Turkey.

It should also be understood that China and Russia are (unofficially) allies of Iran, supplying them with advanced military equipment and a sophisticated missile defense system. While both countries have endorsed the sanctions regime directed against Iran under UN Security Council Resolution 1929 (June 2010), it is unlikely that China and Russia will take on a passive position if and when the aerial bombardments against Iran are carried out.

The new pre-emptive nuclear doctrine calls for the integration of "defensive" and "offensive" operations. Moreover, the important distinction between conventional and nuclear weapons has been blurred. From a military standpoint, the US and its coalition partners including Israel and Turkey are in "a state of readiness". Through media disinformation, the objective is to galvanize Western public opinion in support of a US-led war on Iran in retaliation for Iran's defiance of the international community.

War propaganda consists in fabricating an enemy while conveying the illusion that the Western world is under attack by Islamic terrorists, who are directly supported by the Tehran government.

The national security slogans are:

"Make the world safer."

"Prevent the proliferation of dirty nuclear devices by terrorists."

"Implement punitive actions against Iran to ensure the peace."

"Combat nuclear proliferation by rogue states."

NOTES

1. A. Robock, L. Oman, G. L. Stenchikov, O. B. Toon, C. Bardeen, and R. P. Turco, "Climatic consequences of regional nuclear conflicts", *Atmospheric Chemistry and Physics*, 7, 2003–2012, 2007, http://climate.envsci.rutgers.edu/pdf/acp-7-2003-2007.pdf.

2. US Department of Defense, Nuclear Posture Review, Washington DC, submitted to the US Congress on 31 December 2001, see http://www.globalresearch.ca/index.php?context=va&aid=11921.

3. *Defense Daily*, 12 November 2002.

4. Alice Slater, "Bush Nuclear Policy a Recipe for National Insecurity", *Global Research*, http://globalresearch.ca/articles/SLA308A.html, 14 August 2003.

5. Julian Borger quoting Pentagon Representative Major Michael Shavers, "'Dr Strangeloves' meet to plan new nuclear era", *The Guardian*, http://www.guardian.co.uk/world/2003/aug/07/usa.julianborger, 7 August 2003.

6. *The Guardian*, 31 July 2003.

7. Secretary of Energy Advisory Board, "Recommendations for the Nuclear Weapons Complex of the Future", Report of the Nuclear Weapons Complex Infrastructure Task Force, U.S. Department of Energy, Washington DC, http://www.globalsecurity.org/wmd/library/report/2005/nwcitf-rept_13jul2005.pdf, 13 July 2005.

8. *Ibid.*

9. *Ibid.*

10. *Ibid.*

11. *Ibid.*

12. National Security Strategy, The White House, http://www.whitehouse.gov/nsc/nss.html, Washington DC, 2002.

13. Quoted in Hans M. Kristensen, "The Nuclear Posture of the United States", Federation of American Scientists, http://www.fas.org/programs/ssp/nukes/publications1/Article_NUPI2008.pdf, p. 60, 2008.

14. CIA Intelligence Directorate, "Terrorist CBRN: Materials and Effects", Central Intelligence Agency, https://www.cia.gov/library/reports/general-reports1/terrorist_cbrn/terrorist_CBRN.htm, June 2003. See also *Washington Times*, June 3, 2003.

15. Michel Chossudovsky, "Who is Osama bin Laden?", *Global Research*, http://www.globalresearch.ca/index.php?context=viewArticle&code=20010912&articleId=368, 12 September 2001.

16. Condoleezza Rice, Statement to the Senate Budget Committee, 16 February 2006.

17. US Department of Defense, "The 2010 Nuclear Posture Review", http://www.de fcnsc.gov/npr/docs/2010%20Nuclear%20Posture%20Review%20Report.pdf, Washington DC, April 2010.

18. *Ibid.*, p. iv, italics added.

19. *Ibid.*, p. v-vi, italics added.

20. Joint Chiefs of Staff, "Doctrine for Joint Nuclear Operations", Joint Publication 3-12, http://zfacts.com/metaPage/lib/zFacts_2005_03_15_Joint_Nuclear_Operations.pdf, Washington DC, March 2005.

21. *Ibid.*, italics added.

22. See also the report of the Project for the New American Century (PNAC), "Rebuilding America's Defenses: Strategy, Forces and Resources for a New Century", http://www.newamericancentury.org/RebuildingAmericasDefenses.pdf, Washington DC, September 2000.

23. Joint Chiefs of Staff, "Doctrine for Joint Nuclear Operations", Joint Publication 3-12, *op. cit.*, http://zfacts.com/metaPage/lib/zFacts_2005_03_15_Joint_Nuclear_Operations.pdf, Washington DC, March 2005, italics added.

24. *Ibid.*, p. III-1, italics added.

25. NSPD-17 / HSPD 4, "National Strategy to Combat Weapons of Mass Destruction", unclassified version, The White House, http://www.fas.org/irp/offdocs/nspd/nspd-wmd.pdf, Washington DC, December 2002.

26. Joint Chiefs of Staff, "Doctrine for Joint Nuclear Operations", Joint Publication 3-12, *op. cit.*, p. 47, http://zfacts.com/metaPage/lib/zFacts_2005_03_15_Joint_Nuclear_Operations.pdf, Washington DC, March 2005, italics added. For further details see Michel Chossudovsky, "Nuclear War against Iran", *Global Research*, http://www.globalresearch.ca/index.php?context=viewArticle&code=20060217&articleId=1988, 3 January 2006.

27. Joint Chiefs of Staff, "Doctrine for Joint Nuclear Operations", Joint Publication 3-12, *op. cit.*, http://zfacts.com/metaPage/lib/zFacts_2005_03_15_Joint_Nuclear_Operations.pdf, Washington DC, March 2005, italics added.

28. *Ibid.*

29. Michel Chossudovsky, "The Dangers of a Middle East Nuclear War", *Global Research*, http://www.globalresearch.ca/index.php?context=viewArticle&code=20060217&articleId=1988, 17 February 2006.

30. For further details see Michel Chossudovsky, "Nuclear War against Iran", *Global Research,* http://www.globalresearch.ca/index.php?context=viewArticle&code=%20CH20060103&articleId=1714, 6 January 2006.

31. Philip Giraldi, "Attack on Iran: Pre-emptive Nuclear War", *The American Conservative,* http://www.globalresearch.ca/index.php?context=viewArticle&code=20050802&

articleId=791, 2 August 2005.

32. *Ibid.*

33. Michael Keefer, "Petrodollars and Nuclear Weapons Proliferation: Understanding the Planned Assault on Iran", *Global Research,* http://www.globalresearch.ca/index.php?context=viewArticle&code=KEE20060210&articleId=1936, 10 February 2006.

34. Robert S. Norris and Hans M. Kristensen, "U.S. Nuclear Forces", Bulletin of the Atomic Scientists, 62: 68-71, http://bos.sagepub.com/content/62/1/68.full, January 2006.

35. *Japanese Economic Newswire,* 30 December 2005.

36. According to Hans Kristensen of the Nuclear Information Project, quoted in *Japanese Economic News Wire, op. cit.*

37. See Hans Kristensen, "STRATCOM Cancels Controversial Preemption Strike Plan", *FAS Strategic Security Blog,* No. 169, http://www.fas.org/blog/ssp/2008/07/global strike.php.

38. U.S. Strategic Command, Fact Sheets, http://www.stratcom.mil/factsheets/gs, current as of November 2007.

39. Ibrahim Karagul, "The US is Deploying Nuclear Weapons in Iraq Against Iran", YeniSafak.com, quoted in BBC Monitoring Europe, 20 December 2005.

40. For further details see Michel Chossudovsky, "Nuclear War against Iran", *Global Research,* http://www.globalresearch.ca/index.php?context=viewArticle&code=%20CH20060103&articleId=1714, 6 January 2006.

41. *Washington Post,* 6 January 2006.

42. *Reuters,* 26 April 2005.

43. *Reuters,* 21 September 2004.

44. Peter Beaumont, "Israel deploys nuclear arms in submarines", *The Observer,* http://www.guardian.co.uk/world/2003/oct/12/israel1, 12 October 2003.

45. *Newsweek,* 13 February 2006. See also CDI Database, http://www.cdi.org/issues/nukef&f/database/nukearsenals.cfm.

46. National Resources Defense Council, "U.S. Nuclear Weapons in Europe", http://www.nrdc.org/nuclear/euro/contents.asp, February 2005.

47. Eben Harrell, "NATO Ponders What to Do with its Nuclear Weapons", *Time Magazine,* http://www.time.com/time/world/article/0,8599,2024161,00.html, 7 October 2010.

48. Quoted in National Resources Defense Council, "U.S. Nuclear Weapons in Europe", *op. cit.,* http://www.nrdc.org/nuclear/euro/contents.asp, February 2005.

49. Quoted in The Nuclear Information Project, http://www.nukestrat.com/us/afn/nato.htm, 2005, italics added.

Chapter III
AMERICA'S HOLY CRUSADE
──────── AND ────────
THE BATTLE FOR OIL

US military dogma and war propaganda under the Bush Administration were predicated on combating Islamic fundamentalism rather than targeting Muslims. They propagated the myth that this is not a war between the West and Islam, but a war against terrorism. So-called "Good Muslims" are to be distinguished from "Bad Muslims".

> The dust from the collapse of the twin towers had hardly settled on 11 September 2001 when the febrile search began for "moderate Muslims", people who would provide answers, who would distance themselves from this outrage and condemn the violent acts of "Muslim extremists", "Islamic fundamentalists" and "Islamists". Two distinct categories of Muslims rapidly emerged: the "good" and the "bad"; the "moderates", "liberals" and "secularists" versus the "fundamentalists", the "extremists" and the "Islamists".[1]

In the wake of 9/11, the Muslim community in most Western countries was markedly on the defensive. The "Good Muslim"/"Bad Muslim" divide was broadly accepted. The 9/11 terrorist attacks allegedly perpetrated by Muslims were not only condemned, Muslim communities also supported the US-NATO invasion and occupation of Afghanistan, as part of a legitimate campaign directed against Islamic fundamentalism. Washington's objective was to instill a sentiment of guilt within the Muslim community. The fact that the 9/11 attacks were not instigated by Muslims has rarely been acknowledged by the Muslim community. Al Qaeda's ongoing relationship to the CIA, its role as a US-sponsored "intelligence asset" going back to the Soviet-Afghan war is not mentioned.[2]

Since the early 1980s, Washington has covertly supported the most conservative and fundamentalist factions of Islam, largely with a view to weakening secular, nationalist and progressive movements in the Middle East and Central Asia.

Known and documented, the fundamentalist Wahhabi and Salafi missions from Saudi Arabia, dispatched not only to Afghanistan but also to the Balkans and to the Muslim republics of the former Soviet republics, were covertly supported by US intelligence.[3] What is often referred to as "Political Islam" is in large part a creation of the US intelligence apparatus (with the support of Britain's MI6 and Israel's Mossad).

Beneath the political smokescreen, the distinction between "Good Muslims" and "Bad Muslims" is being scrapped. The "Global War on Terrorism" (GWOT) directed against Al Qaeda and launched in the wake of 9/11 is evolving towards a full-fledged "war of religion", a holy crusade directed against the Muslim World. Supported by the Western media, a generalized atmosphere of racism and xenophobia directed against Muslims has unfolded, particularly in Western Europe, which provides a fake legitimacy to the US war agenda. The latter is upheld as a "Just War". The "Just War" theory serves to camouflage the nature of US war plans, while providing a human face to the invaders.

Going after "Islamic terrorists", carrying out a worldwide pre-emptive war to "protect the homeland", are used to justify a military agenda. The Global War on Terrorism is presented as a "clash of civilizations", a war between competing values and religions, when in reality it is an outright war of conquest, guided by strategic and economic objectives.

The GWOT is the ideological backbone of the American Empire. It defines US military doctrine, including the pre-emptive use of nuclear weapons against the state sponsors of terrorism. The pre-emptive "defensive war" doctrine and the "war on terrorism" against Al Qaeda constitute essential building blocks of America's National Security Strategy as formulated in early 2002. The goal is to incite "pre-emptive military action" out of so-called "self-defense" against two categories of enemies, "rogue states" and "Islamic terrorists", which they claim have weapons of mass destruction.

The logic of the "outside enemy" and the evildoer, allegedly responsible for civilian deaths, prevails over common sense. In the inner consciousness of Americans, the attacks of September 11, 2001 justify acts of war and conquest:

> As was demonstrated by the losses on September 11, 2001, mass civilian casualties is the specific objective of terrorists and these losses would be exponentially more severe if terrorists acquired and used weapons of mass destruction.[4]

The "Global War on Terrorism", increasingly upheld as a "war of religion", justifies a mammoth defense budget at the expense not only of health and education, but of virtually every single category of public expenditure.

America's Crusade in Central Asia and the Middle East

The "Global War on Terrorism" requires going after the perceived terrorists using advanced weapons systems. It upholds a pre-emptive religious-like crusade against evil, which serves to obscure the real objectives of military action. The lies underlying 9/11 are known and documented. The American people's acceptance of this crusade against evil is not based on any rational understanding or analysis of the facts. America's inquisition is used to extend America's sphere of influence and justify military intervention, as part of an international campaign against "Islamic terrorists". Its ultimate objective, which is never mentioned in press reports, is territorial conquest and control over strategic resources.

The objective of the "Global War on Terrorism" launched in September 2001 is to galvanize public support for a worldwide campaign against heresy. America's campaign against evil has been enunciated and carefully formulated by Washington's neoconservative think tanks. It is carried out by the military-intelligence establishment. It is embodied in presidential speeches and press conferences:

> We've been warned *there are evil people in this world*.
> We've been warned so vividly.... And we'll be alert. Your

government is alert. The governors and mayors are alert that evil folks still lurk out there. As I said yesterday, people have declared war on America and they have made a terrible mistake... My administration has a job to do and we're going to do it. We will rid the world of the evil-doers.[5]

In the eyes of public opinion, possessing a "just cause" for waging war is central. A war is said to be just if it is waged on moral, religious or ethical grounds.

America's crusade in Central Asia and the Middle East is no exception. The "war on terrorism" purports to defend the American Homeland and protect the "civilized world". It is upheld as a "war of religion", a "clash of civilizations", when in fact the main objective of this war is to secure control and corporate ownership over the region's extensive oil wealth, while also imposing under the helm of the IMF and the World Bank, the privatization of state enterprises and the transfer of the countries' economic assets into the hands of foreign capital.

The Just War theory upholds war as a "humanitarian operation". It serves to camouflage the real objectives of the military operation, while providing a moral and principled image to the invaders.

Possessing a "just cause" for waging war is central to the Bush Administration's justification for invading and occupying both Afghanistan and Iraq. Taught in US military academies, a modern-day version of the "Just War" theory has been embodied into US military doctrine. The "war on terrorism" and the notion of "pre-emption" are predicated on the right to "self defense." They define "when it is permissible to wage war": *jus ad bellum*.

Jus ad bellum serves to build a consensus within the Armed Forces command structures. It also serves to convince the troops that the enemy is "evil" and that they are fighting for a "just cause". More generally, the Just War theory in its modern day version is an integral part of war propaganda and media disinformation, applied to gain public support for a war agenda. The objective is to instill fear, rouse and harness citizens' unbending support for the next stage of America's "long war", which consists in waging "humanitarian" aerial attacks on the Islamic Republic of Iran, portrayed by the media as endorsing the terrorists. While "all Muslims are not terrorists", all terrorist attacks (planned or realized) are reported by the media as being perpetrated by Muslims.

In America, the Muslim community as a whole is being targeted. Islam is described as a "religion of war". The proposed mosque and community center close to Ground Zero are being heralded as "violating the sanctity of Ground Zero":

> Opening a mosque at Ground Zero is offensive and disrespectful to the city and the people who died in the attacks. The project is "spitting in the face of everyone murdered on 9/11.[6]

"Homegrown Terrorists"

The arrests on trumped up charges, as well as the show trials of alleged "homegrown" "Islamic terrorists", perform an important function. They sustain the illusion in the inner consciousness of Americans that "Islamic terrorists" not only constitute a real threat but that the Muslim community to which they belong is broadly supportive of their actions:

> The threat increasingly comes not from strangers with rough English and dubious passports. Instead, it resides much closer to home: in urban townhouses, darkened basements – anywhere with an Internet connection. Homegrown terrorism is the latest incarnation of the al-Qaeda threat.[7]

From a process of selective targeting of Muslims with radical tendencies (or allegedly associated with "terrorist organizations"), what is now unfolding is a generalized process of demonization of an entire population group. Muslims are increasingly the object of routine discrimination and ethnic profiling. They are considered a potential threat to national security. The threat is said to be "much closer to home", "within your neighborhood". In other words what is unfolding is an all out witch-hunt reminiscent of the Spanish Inquisition.

In turn, Al Qaeda is described as a powerful multinational terrorist organization (possessing WMDs) with "subsidiaries" in a number of Muslim countries, and that it is present (with corresponding acronyms) in various geopolitical hotspots and war theaters: Al Qaeda in Iraq (AQI), Al Qaeda in the Arabian Peninsula (AQAP) (comprised of Al Qaeda in Saudi Arabia and the Islamic Jihad of Yemen), Al Qaeda in Southeast Asia (Jamaah Islamiyah), Al-Qaeda Organization in the Islamic Maghreb, Harakat al-Shabaab Mujahideen in Somalia, the Egyptian Islamic Jihad, etc.

At no moment is the issue of atrocities committed against several million Muslims in Iraq and Afghanistan considered a terrorist act by the occupation forces.

The American Inquisition

A "war of religion" is unfolding, with a view to justifying a global military crusade. In the inner consciousness of many Americans, the "holy crusade" against Muslims is justified. While President Obama may uphold freedom of religion, the US inquisitorial social order has institutionalized patterns of discrimination, prejudice and xenophobia directed against Muslims. Ethnic profiling applies to travel, the job market, access to education and social services and more generally to social status and mobility.

The American Inquisition is an ideological construct which is, in many regards, similar to the inquisitorial social order prevailing in France and Spain during the Middle Ages. The inquisition, which started in France in the 12th century, was used as a justification for conquest and military intervention.[8]

The arrests, trials and sentences of so-called "homegrown terrorists" (from within America's Muslim community) on trumped up charges sustain the legitimacy of the Homeland Security State and its inquisitorial legal and law enforcement apparatus.

An inquisitorial doctrine turns realities upside down. It is a social order based on lies and fabrications. But because these lies emanate from the highest political authority and are part of a widely held "consensus", they invariably remain unchallenged. And those who challenge the inquisitorial social order or in any way oppose America's military or national security agenda are themselves branded as "conspiracy theorists" or outright terrorists.

Washington's Extrajudicial Assassination Program

Beyond the process of inquisitorial arrests and prosecution, an expedient extrajudicial assassination program sanctioned by the White House has been launched. This program, which outshines the Spanish Inquisition, allows US special forces to kill American citizens and suspected homegrown terrorists.[9]
The legitimacy of the inquisition is not questioned.

The objective is to sustain the illusion that America is under attack and that Muslims across the land are complicit and supportive of "Islamic terrorism". The demonization of Muslims sustains a global military agenda. Under the American Inquisition, Washington has a self-proclaimed holy mandate to extirpate Islam and "spread democracy" throughout the world.

What we are dealing with is an outright and blind acceptance of the structures of power and political authority. America's holy crusade against the Muslim World is an outright criminal act directed against millions of people. It is a war of economic conquest.

The Battle for Oil

More than sixty percent of the world's oil and natural gas reserves lie in Muslim lands. "The Battle for Oil" waged by the US-NATO-Israel military alliance requires the demonization of the inhabitants of those countries which possess these vast reserves of oil and natural gas.[10] Iran possesses ten percent of global oil and gas reserves. The US is the first and foremost military and nuclear power in the world, but it possesses less than two percent of global oil and gas reserves.

The "war on terrorism" and the hate campaign directed against Muslims bears a direct relationship to the "Battle for Middle East Oil". How best to conquer these vast oil reserves located in countries inhabited by Muslims? Build a political consensus against Muslim countries, describe them as "uncivilized", denigrate their culture and religion, implement ethnic profiling against Muslims in Western countries, and foster hatred and racism against the inhabitants of the oil producing countries.

The values of Islam are said to be tied into "Islamic terrorism". Western governments are now accusing Iran of "exporting terrorism to the West". In the words of former Prime Minister Tony Blair:

> There is a virus of extremism which comes out of the cocktail of religious fanaticism and political repression in the Middle East which is now being exported to the rest of the world. We will only secure our future if we are dealing with every single aspect of that problem. Our future security depends on sorting out the stability of that region. You can never say never in any of these situations.[11]

Muslims are demonized, casually identified with "Islamic terrorists", who are also described as constituting a nuclear threat. In turn, the terrorists are supported by Iran, an Islamic Republic which threatens the "civilized world" with deadly nuclear weapons (which it does not possess). In contrast, America's "humanitarian" nuclear weapons will be "accurate, safe and reliable".

The US-led war in the broader Middle East Central Asian region consists in gaining control over more than sixty percent of the world's reserves of oil and natural gas. The Anglo-American oil giants also seek to gain control over oil and gas pipeline routes out of the region. Muslim countries including Saudi Arabia, Iraq, Iran, Kuwait, the United Arab Emirates, Qatar, Yemen, Libya, Nigeria, Algeria, Kazakhstan, Azerbaijan, Malaysia, Indonesia, Brunei, possess between 66.2 and 75.9 percent of total oil reserves, depending on the source and methodology of the estimate. (See Table 3.1 below.)

In contrast, the United States of America has barely two percent of total oil reserves. Western countries including its major oil producers (Canada, the US, Norway, the UK, Denmark and Australia) control approximately four percent of total oil reserves. (In the alternative estimate of the *Oil & Gas Journal* which includes Canada's oil sands, this percentage would be of the order of 16.5 percent.) (See table below.)

The largest share of the world's oil reserves lies in a region extending (North) from the tip of Yemen to the Caspian Sea basin and (East) from the Eastern Mediterranean coastline to the Persian Gulf. This broader Middle East-Central Asian region, which is the theater of the US-led "war on terrorism" encompasses, according to the estimates of *World Oil*, more than sixty percent of the World's oil reserves. (See Table 3.1 below.)

Iraq has five times more oil than the United States. Muslim countries possess at least sixteen times more oil than the Western countries combined. The major non-Muslim oil reserve countries are Venezuela, Russia, Mexico, China and Brazil.

Demonization is applied to an enemy which possesses three-quarters of the world's oil reserves. "Axis of evil", "rogue states", "failed nations", "Islamic terrorists": demonization and vilification are the ideological pillars of America's "war on terror". They serve as a *casus belli* for waging the battle for oil.

The Battle for Oil requires the demonization of those who possess the oil. The enemy is characterized as evil, with a view to justifying military action including the mass killing of civilians. The Middle East Central Asian region is heavily militarized. The oil fields are encircled by NATO war ships stationed in the Eastern Mediterranean (as part of a UN "peacekeeping" operation), US Carrier Strike Groups and Destroyer Squadrons in the Persian Gulf and the Arabian Sea deployed as part of the "war on terrorism". The ultimate objective, combining military action, covert intelligence operations and war propaganda, is to break down the national fabric and transform sovereign countries into open economic territories, where natural resources can be plundered and confiscated under "free market" supervision. This control also extends to strategic oil and gas pipeline corridors (e.g. Afghanistan).

Demonization is a psy-op, used to sway public opinion and build a consensus in favor of war. Psychological warfare is directly sponsored by the Pentagon and the US intelligence apparatus. It is not limited to assassinating or executing the rulers of Muslim countries; it extends to entire populations. It also targets Muslims in Western Europe and North America. It purports to break national consciousness and the ability to resist the invader. It denigrates Islam. It creates social divisions. It is intended to divide national societies and ultimately trigger "civil war". While it creates an environment which facilitates the outright appropriation of the countries' resources, at the same time, it potentially backlashes, creates a new national

Table 3.1 Proven reserves in billions of barrels

RANK	COUNTRY	PERCENT OF WORLD RESERVES	WORLD OIL, DECEMBER 2004	PERCENT OF WORLD RESERVES	OIL & GAS JOURNAL, JANUARY 2006
1.	Saudi Arabia	24.2	262.1	20.6	266.8
2.	Canada*	0.4	4.7	13.8	178.8
3.	Iran	12.1	130.8	10.3	132.5
4.	Iraq	10.6	115.0	8.9	115.0
5.	Kuwait	9.2	99.7	7.9	101.5
6.	United Arab Emirates	6.5	69.9	7.6	97.8
7.	Venezuela*	4.8	52.4	6.1	79.7
8.	Russia	6.2	67.1	4.6	60.0
9.	Libya	3.2	33.6	3.0	39.1
10.	Nigeria	3.4	36.6	2.7	35.9
11.	United States	2.0	21.4	1.7	21.4
12.	China	1.4	15.4	1.4	18.3
13.	Qatar	1.8	20	1.2	15.2
14.	Mexico	1.4	14.8	1.0	12.9
15.	Algeria	1.4	15.3	0.9	11.4
16.	Brazil	1.0	11.2	0.9	11.2
17.	Kazakhstan	0.8	9.0	0.7	9.0
18.	Norway	0.9	9.9	0.6	7.7
19.	Azerbaijan	0.6	7.0	0.5	7.0
20.	India	0.5	4.9	0.4	5.8
21	Oman	0.4.	4.8	0.4	5.5
22	Angola	0.8.	9.0	0.4	5.4
23	Ecuador	0.5	5.5	0.4	4.6
24	Indonesia	0.5	5.3	0.3	4.3
25	UK	0.4	3.9	0.3	4.0
26	Yemen	0.3	3.0	0.3	4.0
27	Egypt	0.3	3.6	0.3	3.7
28	Malaysia	0.3	3.0	0.2	3.0
29	Gabon	0.2	2.2	0.2	2.5
30	Syria	0.2	2.3	0.2	2.5
31	Argentina	0.2	2.3	0.2	2.3
32	Equatorial Guinea	0.2	1,8	0.0	0.0
32	Colombia	0.1	1.5	0.1	1.5
33	Vietnam	0.1	1,3		0.6
34	Chad	0.0	0.0	0.1	1.5
35	Australia	0.3	3.6	0.1	1.4
36	Brunei	0.1	1.1	0.1	1.4
37	Denmark	0.1	1.3	0.1	1.3
38	Peru	0.1	0.9	0.1	1.0
Total Muslim Countries**		75.9	822.1	66.2	855.6
Total Western World (EU, North America, Australia)		4.1	44.8	16.5	213.3
Other Countries		20.6	214.9	17.3	223.6
World Total 100.0		100.0	1,081.8	100.0	1,292.5

Source: *EIO: Energy Information Administration* (See next page for explanatory notes on the table.)

consciousness, develops inter-ethnic solidarity, and brings people together in confronting the invaders.

It is worth noting that the triggering of sectarian divisions and "civil wars" is contemplated in the process of redrawing the map of the Middle East, where countries are slated to be broken up and transformed into territories. The map of the New Middle East, although not official, has been used by the US National War Academy. It was recently published in the *Armed Forces Journal* (June 2006). In this map, nation states are broken up; international borders are redefined along sectarian-ethnic lines, broadly in accordance with the interests of the Anglo-American oil giants. The map has also been used in a training program at NATO's Defense College for senior military officers.[12]

The Oil Lies in Muslim Lands

The oil lies in Muslim lands. Vilification of the enemy is part and parcel of Eurasia energy geopolitics. It is a direct function of the geographic distribution of the world's oil and gas reserves. If the oil were in countries occupied predominantly by Buddhists or Hindus,

---

Note on Table 3.1:

Indicated are the world's main oil reserve countries. Countries with less than 0.1 percent of total reserves are not indicated.

The *Oil & Gas Journal* figures indicated above are based on proven oil reserves including the bituminous oil fields (oil sands or tar sands). The world oil figures indicate oil reserves without the tar sands. The difference between the two sets of figures largely pertains to the position of Canada and Venezuela. The tar-sands are considered by some experts as not recoverable with present technology and prices, although this issue is the object of heated debate.

Muslim countries are indicated in **bold**. Percentages are rounded up to first decimal.

*Canada appears, according to this estimate, as the second country in terms of the size of proven reserves, due to the size of its bituminous oil fields. The *Oil & Gas Journal*'s oil reserve estimate above for Canada includes 4.7 billion barrels of conventional crude oil and condensate reserves and 174.1 billion barrels of oil sands reserves.

In other recognized estimates, where the oil sands are not accounted for, Canada's reserves are much lower (in billions of barrels), respectively for the years indicated:

BP Statistical Review 16.802

Oil & Gas Journal 178.792

World Oil 4.700

BP notes that "the figure for Canadian oil reserves includes an official estimate of Canadian oil sands 'under active development'" (See BP Statistical Review of World Energy 2006,

http://www.investis.com/bp_acc_ia/stat_review_05/htdocs/reports/report_1.html). BP says of its data sources for oil reserves that "the estimates in this table have been compiled using a combination of primary official sources, third-party data from the OPEC Secretariat, *World Oil*, *Oil & Gas Journal* and an independent estimate of Russian reserves based on information in the public domain" (See BP website,

http://www.bp.com/sectiongenericarticle.do?categoryId=9023809&contentId=7044537). *World Oil*'s Canadian oil reserve estimate "does not include 174 billion bbl [barrels] of oil sands reserves."[14]

one would expect that US foreign policy would be directed against Buddhists and Hindus, who would also be the object of vilification.

In the Middle East war theater, Iran and Syria, which are part of the "axis of evil", are the next targets according to official US statements. US sponsored "civil wars" have also been conducted in several other strategic oil and gas regions including Nigeria, the Sudan, Colombia, Somalia, Yemen, Angola, not to mention Chechnya and several republics of the former Soviet Union. Ongoing US-sponsored "civil wars", which often include the channeling of covert support to paramilitary groups, have been triggered in the Darfur region of Sudan as well as in Somalia, Darfur possesses extensive oil reserves. In Somalia, lucrative concessions have already been granted to four Anglo-American oil giants.

> According to documents obtained by *The Times*, nearly two-thirds of Somalia was allocated to the American oil giants Conoco, Amoco [now part of BP], Chevron and Phillips in the final years before Somalia's pro-U.S. President Mohamed Siad Barre was overthrown and the nation plunged into chaos in January, 1991. Industry sources said the companies holding the rights to the most promising concessions are hoping that the Bush Administration's decision to send U.S. troops to safeguard aid shipments to Somalia will also help protect their multimillion-dollar investments there.[13]

Globalization and the Conquest of the World's Energy Resources

The collective demonization of Muslims, including the vilification of Islam, applied worldwide, constitutes at the ideological level an instrument of conquest of the world's energy resources. It is part of the broader economic and political mechanisms underlying the New World Order.

NOTES

1. Tariq Ramadan, "Good Muslim, Bad Muslim", *New Statesman,* http://www.new statesman.com/religion/2010/02/muslim-religious-moderation, 12 February 2010.

2. Michel Chossudovsky, *America's "War on Terrorism"*, Chapter II, Global Research

Publishers, Montreal, 2005.

3. *Ibid.*

4. National Security Strategy, White House, Washington DC, 2002, *op. cit.*

5. George W. Bush, CNN, 16 September 2001, italics added.

6. Jodi Lai, "Plan to build mosque at Ground Zero angers New Yorkers", *National Post,* http://news.nationalpost.com/2010/05/17/plan-to-build-mosque-atground-zero-angers-new-yorkers/, 17 May 2010.

7. Andrew Duffy, "How terror came home to roost", *Ottawa Citizen,* http://www.ot tawacitizen.com/news/Analysis+terror+came+home+roost/3452693/story.html, 27 August 2010.

8. Michel Chossudovsky, "9/11 and the 'American Inquisition'", *Global Research,* http://www.globalresearch.ca/index.php?context=va&aid=10144, 11 September 2008.

9. Chuck Norris, "Obama's US Assassination Program? 'A Shortlist of U.S. Citizens Specifically Targeted for Killing?'", *Global Research,* http://globalresearch.ca/index.php?context=va&aid=20779, 26 August 2010.

10. Michel Chossudovsky, "The Demonization of Muslims and the Battle for Oil", *Global Research,* http://globalresearch.ca/index.php?context=va&aid=4347, 4 January 2007.

11. *The Mirror,* London, 7 February 2006.

12. Mahdi Darius Nazemroaya, "Plans for Redrawing the Middle East: The Project for a "New Middle East"", *Global Research,* http://www.globalresearch.ca/index.php?con text=va&aid=3882, 18 November 2006.

13. Mark Fineman, "The Oil Factor in Somalia: Four American Petroleum Giants had Agreements with the African Nation Before its Civil War Began", *Los Angeles Times,* 18 January 1993.

14. *Ibid.*

CHAPTER IV
PREPARING FOR
─────── WORLD WAR THREE ───────

Humanity is at a dangerous crossroads. War preparations to attack Iran are in an advanced state of readiness. Hi-tech weapons systems including nuclear warheads are fully deployed.

This military adventure has been on the Pentagon's drawing board since the mid-1990s: first Iraq, then Iran, according to a declassified 1995 US Central Command document.

Escalation is part of the military agenda. While Iran is the next target together with Syria and Lebanon, this strategic military deployment also threatens North Korea, China and Russia.

Since 2005, the US and its allies, including America's NATO partners and Israel, have been involved in the extensive deployment and stockpiling of advanced weapons systems.

The air defense systems of the US-NATO member countries and Israel are fully integrated.

This is a coordinated endeavor of the Pentagon, NATO, Israel's Defense Force (IDF), with the active military involvement of several non-NATO partner countries including the frontline Arab states (members of NATO's Mediterranean Dialogue and the Istanbul Cooperation Initiative), Saudi Arabia, Japan, South Korea, India, Indonesia, Singapore and Australia, among others.

NATO consists of 28 NATO member states. Another 21 countries are members of the Euro-Atlantic Partnership Council (EAPC), The Mediterranean Dialogue and the Istanbul Cooperation Initiative include ten Arab countries plus Israel.

In post-9/11 military doctrine, this massive deployment of military hardware has been defined as part of the so-called "Global War on Terrorism", targeting "non-state" terrorist organizations including al Qaeda and so-called "state sponsors of terrorism", including Iran, Syria, Lebanon and Sudan. The setting up of new US-NATO military bases, the stockpiling of advanced weapons systems including tactical nuclear weapons, etc., were implemented as part of the preemptive defensive military doctrine as well as in the context of NATO's new 2010 Strategic Concept.[1]

The roles of Egypt, the Gulf states and Saudi Arabia (within the extended military alliance) are of particular relevance. Egypt controls the transit of war ships and oil tankers through the Suez Canal. Saudi Arabia and the Gulf states occupy the South Western coastlines of the Persian Gulf, the Straits of Hormuz and the Gulf of Oman.

In June 2010, following the adoption of renewed sanctions directed against Iran by the UN Security Council, Egypt allowed Israeli and US warships to pass through the Suez Canal in "an apparent signal to Iran... [In June 2010 Saudi Arabia] granted Israel the right to fly over its airspace..."[2]

Media Disinformation

Public opinion, swayed by media hype, is tacitly supportive, indifferent or ignorant as to the likely impacts of what is upheld as an *ad hoc* "punitive" operation directed against Iran's nuclear facilities rather than an all-out war. War preparations include the deployment of US and Israeli-produced nuclear weapons. In this context, the devastating consequences of a nuclear war are either trivialized or simply not mentioned.

The "real crisis" threatening humanity, according to the media and the governments, is not war but global warming. The media will fabricate a crisis where there is no crisis: "a global scare" – the H1N1 global pandemic – but nobody seems to fear a US-sponsored nuclear war.

The war on Iran is presented to public opinion as an issue among others. It is not viewed as a threat to "Mother Earth" as in the case of global warming. It is not front-page news. The fact that an attack on Iran could lead to escalation and potentially unleash a "global war" is not a matter of concern.

A "Pre-emptive" Aerial Attack Directed Against Iran would Lead to Escalation

At present there are three separate Middle East/Central Asia war theaters: Iraq, Af-Pak and Palestine. Were Iran to be the object of a "pre-emptive" aerial attack by allied forces, the entire region, from the Eastern Mediterranean to China's Western frontier with Afghanistan and Pakistan, would flare up, leading us potentially into a World War III scenario. The war would also extend into Lebanon and Syria.

It is highly unlikely that the bombings, if they were to be implemented, would be circumscribed to Iran's nuclear facilities as claimed by US-NATO official statements. What is more probable is an all-out air attack on both military and civilian infrastructure, transport systems, factories and public buildings.

The oil reserves of the US are estimated at less than 20 billion barrels. The broader region of the Middle East and Central Asia have oil reserves which are more than thirty times those of the US, representing more than sixty percent of the world's total reserves.[3] Of significance is the recent discovery in Iran of the second largest known reserves of natural gas at Soumar and Halgan, estimated at 12.4 trillion cubic feet.

Targeting Iran consists not only in reclaiming Anglo-American control over Iran's oil and gas economy, including pipeline routes, it also challenges the presence and influence of China and Russia in the region.

The planned attack on Iran is part of a coordinated global military road map. It is part of the Pentagon's "long war", a profit-driven war without borders, a project of World domination, a sequence of military operations.

US-NATO military planners have envisaged various scenarios of military escalation. They are also acutely aware of the geopolitical implications, namely, that the war could extend beyond the Middle East Central Asia region. The economic impacts on the oil markets have also been analyzed.

While Iran, Syria and Lebanon are the immediate targets, China, Russia, North Korea, not to mention Venezuela and Cuba, are also the object of US threats.

At stake is the structure of military alliances. US-NATO-Israel military deployments including military exercises and drills conducted on Russia and China's immediate borders bear a direct relationship to the proposed war on Iran. These veiled threats, including their timing, constitute an obvious hint to the former powers of the Cold War era not to intervene in any way which could encroach upon a US-led attack on Iran.

Global Warfare

The medium term strategic objective is to target Iran and neutralize Iran's allies, through gunboat diplomacy. The longer term military objective is to directly target China and Russia.

While Iran is the immediate target, military deployment is by no means limited to the Middle East and Central Asia. A global military agenda has been formulated. The deployment of coalition troops and advanced weapons systems by the US, NATO and its partners is occurring simultaneously in all major regions of the World. The actions of the US military off the coast of North Korea, including the conduct of war games, are part of a global design.

Directed primarily against Russia and China, US, NATO and allied military exercises, war drills, weapons deployments, etc. are being conducted simultaneously in major geopolitical hotspots:

- The Korean Peninsula, the Sea of Japan, the Taiwan Straits, the South China Sea threatening China.

- The deployment of Patriot missiles in Poland, the early warning center in the Czech Republic threatening Russia.

- Naval deployments in Bulgaria, Romania on the Black Sea, threatening Russia.

- US and NATO troop deployments in Georgia.

- A formidable naval deployment in the Persian Gulf including Israeli submarines directed against Iran.

Concurrently, the Eastern Mediterranean, the Black Sea, the Caribbean, Central America and the Andean region of South America are areas of ongoing militarization. In Latin America and the Caribbean, the threats are directed against Venezuela and Cuba.

US "Military Aid"

In turn, large scale weapons transfers have been undertaken under the banner of US "military aid" to selected countries, including a 5-billion dollar arms deal with India which is intended to build India's capabilities directed against China[4]:

> [The] arms sales will improve ties between Washington and New Delhi, and, intentionally or not, will have the effect of containing China's influence in the region.[5]

The US has military cooperation agreements with a number of South East Asian countries including Singapore, Vietnam and Indonesia, involving "military aid" as well as the participation in US-led war games in the Pacific Rim (July-August 2010). These agreements are supportive of weapons deployments directed against The People's Republic of China.[6]

Similarly and more directly related to the planned attack on Iran, the US is arming the Gulf States (Bahrain, Kuwait, Qatar and the United Arab Emirates) with land-based interceptor missiles, Patriot Advanced Capability-3 and Terminal High Altitude Area Defense (THAAD), as well as sea-based Standard Missile-3 interceptors installed on Aegis class warships in the Persian Gulf.[7]

The Timetable of Military Stockpiling and Deployment

What is crucial in regard to US weapons transfers to partner countries and allies is the actual timing of delivery and deployment. The launch of a US-sponsored military operation would normally occur only once these weapons systems are in place, effectively deployed with the implementation of personnel training (e.g. India).

What we are dealing with is a carefully coordinated global military design controlled by the Pentagon, involving the combined armed forces of more than forty countries. This global multinational military deployment is by far the largest display of advanced weapons systems in world history. In turn, the US and its allies have established new military bases in different parts of the world: "The Surface of the Earth is Structured as a Wide Battlefield".[8]

The Unified Command structure divided up into geographic Combatant Commands is predicated on a strategy of militarization at the global level:

> The US Military has bases in 63 countries. Brand new military bases have been built since September 11, 2001 in seven countries. In total, there are 255,065 US military personnel deployed worldwide.[9]

World War III Scenario

"The World Commanders' Areas of Responsibility" defines the Pentagon's global military design, which is one of world conquest. This military deployment is occurring in several regions simultaneously under the coordination of the regional US Commands, involving the stockpiling of US-made weapons systems by US forces and partner countries, some of which are former enemies, including Vietnam and Japan.

The present context is characterized by a global military build-up controlled by one world superpower, which is using its numerous allies to trigger regional wars. In contrast, the Second World War was a conjunction of separate regional war theaters. Given the communications technologies and weapons systems of the 1940s, there was no strategic "real time" coordination in military actions between broad geographic regions. Global warfare is based on the coordinated deployment of a single dominant military power, which oversees the actions of its allies and partners.

With the exception of Hiroshima and Nagasaki, the Second World War was characterized by the use of conventional weapons. The planning of a global war relies on the militarization of outer space. Were a war directed against Iran to be launched, it would not only use nuclear weapons, the entire gamut of new advanced weapons systems, including electrometric weapons and environmental modification techniques (ENMOD) would be used.

The United Nations Security Council

The UN Security Council adopted in June 2010 a fourth round of sweeping sanctions against The Islamic Republic of Iran (UNSC Resolution 1929), which included an expanded arms embargo as well as "tougher financial controls". In a bitter irony, this resolution was passed within days of the United Nations Security Council's outright refusal to adopt a motion condemning Israel for its attack on the Gaza Freedom Flotilla in international waters.

UNSC Resolution 1929 includes an expanded arms embargo as well as "tougher financial controls":

> [Resolution 1929 (June 9, 2010)] decides that all states *shall prevent the direct or indirect supply, sale or transfer to Iran,* from or through their territories or by their nationals or individuals subject to their jurisdiction, or using their flag vessels or aircraft, and whether or not originating in their territories, *of any battle tanks, armoured combat vehicles, large calibre artillery systems, combat aircraft, attack helicopters, warships, missiles or missile systems...* [It] decides further that all states shall prevent the provision to Iran by their nationals or from or through their territories of technical training, financial resources or services, advice, other services or assistance related to the supply, sale, transfer, provision, manufacture, maintenance or use of such arms and related material, and, in this context, calls upon all states to exercise vigilance and restraint over the supply, sale, transfer, provision, manufacture and use of all other arms and related materiel.[10]

Both China and Russia, pressured by the US, have endorsed the UNSC sanctions' regime, to their own detriment. Their decision within the UNSC contributes to weakening their own military alliance, the Shanghai Cooperation organization (SCO), in which Iran has observer status. The Security Council resolution freezes China and Russia's respective bilateral military cooperation and trade agreements with Iran. It has serious repercussions on Iran's air defense system which in part depends on Russian technology and expertise.

In November 2010, following a decree issued by President Dmitry Medvedev, Moscow announced the cancellation of its military cooperation agreement with Iran pertaining to the S300 air defense system.

The UN Security Council Resolution 1929 grants a *de facto* "green light" to wage a pre-emptive war against Iran.

The American Inquisition: Building a Political Consensus for War

In chorus, the Western media has branded Iran as a threat to global security in view of its alleged (non-existent) nuclear weapons program. Echoing official statements, the media is now demanding the implementation of punitive bombings directed against Iran so as to safeguard Israel's security.

The Western media is beating the drums of war. The purpose is to tacitly instill, through repeated media reports, *ad nauseam*, within people's inner consciousness, the notion that the Iranian threat is real and that the Islamic Republic should be "taken out". A consensus-building process to wage war is similar to the Spanish Inquisition. It requires and demands submission to the notion that war is a humanitarian endeavor.

Known and documented, the real threat to global security emanates from the US-NATO-Israel alliance, yet realities in an inquisitorial environment are turned upside down: the warmongers are committed to peace, the victims of war are presented as the protagonists of war. Whereas in 2006, almost two thirds of Americans were opposed to military action against Iran, a Reuter-Zogby February 2010 poll suggests that 56 percent of Americans favor a US-NATO military action against Iran.

Those who are the source of the lie contribute to sustaining the lie.

But there are other factors at work which facilitate the manipulation of public opinion. The antiwar movement in the US, which has in part been infiltrated and co-opted, has taken on a weak stance with regard to Iran. The antiwar movement is divided. The emphasis has been on wars which have already occurred (Afghanistan, Iraq) rather than forcefully opposing wars which are being prepared and which are currently on the Pentagon's drawing board. Since the inauguration of the Obama Administration, the antiwar movement has lost some of its impetus.

Moreover, those who actively oppose the wars on Afghanistan and Iraq, do not necessarily oppose the conduct of "punitive bombings" directed towards Iran, nor do they categorize these bombings as an act of war, which could potentially be a prelude to World War III.

The scale of antiwar protest in relation to Iran has been minimal in comparison to the mass demonstrations which preceded the 2003 bombing and invasion of Iraq.

The real threat to global security emanates from the US-NATO-Israel alliance.

The Iran operation is not being opposed in the diplomatic arena by China and Russia; it has the support of the governments of the frontline Arab states which are integrated into the NATO sponsored Mediterranean dialogue. It also has the tacit support of Western public opinion.

NOTES

1. NATO Strategic Concept, *op. cit.*

2. Muriel Mirak Weissbach, "Israel's Insane War on Iran Must Be Prevented", *Global Research*, http://www.globalresearch.ca/index.php?context=va&aid=20383, 31 July 2010.

3. Eric Waddell, "The Battle for Oil", *Global Research*, http://www.globalresearch.ca/articles/WAD412A.html, 14 December 2004.

4. *Global Times*, "India, US to ink huge military deal: report", *Global Times*, http://world.globaltimes.cn/asia-pacific/2010-07/550830.html, 13 July 2010.

5. Quoted in Rick Rozoff, "Confronting both China and Russia: U.S. Risks Military Clash With China In Yellow Sea", *Global Research*, http://www.globalresearch.ca/index.php?context=va&aid=20149, 16 July 2010.

6. *Ibid.*

7. Rick Rozoff, "NATO's Role in the Military Encirclement of Iran", *Global Research*, http://www.globalresearch.ca/index.php?context=va&aid=17555, 10 February 2010.

8. Jules Dufour, "The Worldwide Network of US Military Bases", *Global Research*, http://www.globalresearch.ca/index.php?context=va&aid=5564, 1 July 2007.

9. *Ibid.*

10. United Nations Security Council, "Security Council Imposes Additional Sanctions

on Iran, Voting 12 in Favour to 2 Against, with 1 Abstention", includes complete text of UNSC Resolution 1929, *UN News,* http://www.un.org/News/Press/docs/2010/sc9948.doc.htm, 9 June 2010, italics added.

Chapter V
TARGETING IRAN
—— WITH NUCLEAR WEAPONS ——

The stockpiling and deployment of advanced weapons systems directed against Iran started in the immediate wake of the 2003 bombing and invasion of Iraq. From the outset, these war plans were led by the US, in liaison with NATO and Israel.

Following the 2003 invasion of Iraq, the Bush administration identified Iran and Syria as the next stage of "the road map to war". US military sources intimated that an aerial attack on Iran could involve a large scale deployment comparable to the US "shock and awe" bombing raids on Iraq in March 2003:

> American air strikes on Iran would vastly exceed the scope of the 1981 Israeli attack on the Osiraq nuclear center in Iraq, and would more resemble the opening days of the 2003 air campaign against Iraq.[1]

Building a Pretext for a Pre-emptive Nuclear Attack

The pretext for waging war on Iran essentially rests on two fundamental premises, which are part of the US administration's National Security doctrine.

1. Iran's alleged possession of "Weapons of Mass Destruction" (WMD), more specifically its alleged nuclear weapons program.

2. Iran's alleged support to "Islamic terrorists".

These are two interrelated statements that are an integral part of the propaganda and media disinformation campaign.

The "Weapons of Mass Destruction (WMD)" statement is used to justify the "pre-emptive war" against the "state sponsors of terror", i.e. countries such as Iran and North Korea, which allegedly possess WMDs. Iran is identified as a state sponsor of so-called "non-state terrorist organizations". The latter allegedly also possess WMDs and potentially constitute a nuclear threat. Terrorist non-state organizations are presented as a "nuclear power".

> The enemies in this [long] war are not traditional conventional military forces but rather dispersed, global terrorist networks that exploit Islam to advance radical political aims. These enemies have the avowed aim of acquiring and using nuclear and biological weapons to murder hundreds of thousands of Americans and others around the world.[2]

In contrast, Germany and Israel, which produce and possess nuclear warheads, are not considered "nuclear powers".

"Theater Iran Near Term"

Code named by US military planners as TIRANNT, "Theater Iran Near Term", simulations of an attack on Iran were initiated in May 2003 "when modelers and intelligence specialists pulled together the data needed for theater-level (meaning large-scale) scenario analysis for Iran."[3]

The scenarios identified several thousand targets inside Iran as part of a "Shock and Awe" Blitzkrieg:

> The analysis, called TIRANNT, for "Theater Iran Near Term," was coupled with a mock scenario for a Marine Corps invasion and a simulation of the Iranian missile force. U.S. and British planners conducted a Caspian Sea war game around the same time. And Bush directed the U.S. Strategic Command to draw up a global strike war plan for an attack against Iranian weapons of mass destruction. All of this will ultimately feed into a new war plan for "major combat operations" against Iran that military sources confirm now [April 2006] exists in draft form...
>
> Under TIRANNT, Army and U.S. Central Command planners have been examining both near-term and out-year scenarios for war with Iran, including all aspects of a major combat operation, from mobilization and deployment of forces through postwar stability operations after regime change.[4]

Different "theater scenarios" for an all out attack on Iran had been contemplated:

> The US army, navy, air force and marines have all prepared battle plans and spent four years building bases and training for 'Operation Iranian Freedom'. Admiral Fallon, the new head of US Central Command, has inherited computerized plans under the name TIRANNT (Theatre Iran Near Term).[5]

In 2004, drawing upon the initial war scenarios under TIRANNT, Vice President Dick Cheney instructed USSTRATCOM to draw up a "contingency plan" of a large-scale military operation directed against Iran "to be employed in response to another 9/11-type terrorist attack on the United States" on the presumption that the government in Tehran would be behind the terrorist plot. The plan included the pre-emptive use of nuclear weapons against a non-nuclear state:

> The plan includes a large-scale air assault on Iran employing both conventional and tactical nuclear weapons. Within Iran there are more than 450 major strategic targets, including numerous suspected nuclear-weapons-program development sites. Many of the targets are hardened or are deep underground and could not be taken out by conventional weapons, hence the nuclear option. As in the case of Iraq, the response is not conditional on Iran actually being involved in the act of terrorism directed against the United States. Several senior Air Force officers involved in the planning are reportedly appalled at the implications of what they are doing – that Iran is being set up for an unprovoked nuclear attack – but no one is prepared to damage his career by posing any objections.[6]

The Military Road Map: "First Iraq, then Iran"

The decision to target Iran under TIRANNT was part of the broader process of military planning and sequencing of military operations. Already under the Clinton administration, US Central Command (USCENTCOM) had formulated "in war theater plans" to invade first Iraq and then Iran. Access to Middle East oil was the stated strategic objective:

The broad national security interests and objectives expressed in the President's National Security Strategy (NSS) and the Chairman's National Military Strategy (NMS) form the foundation of the United States Central Command's theater strategy. The NSS directs implementation of a strategy of dual containment of the rogue states of Iraq and Iran as long as those states pose a threat to U.S. interests, to other states in the region, and to their own citizens. Dual containment is designed to maintain the balance of power in the region without depending on either Iraq or Iran. USCENTCOM's theater strategy is interest-based and threat-focused. The purpose of U.S. engagement, as espoused in the NSS, is to protect the United States' vital interest in the region—uninterrupted, secure U.S./Allied access to Gulf oil.[7]

The war on Iran was viewed as part of a succession of military operations. According to (former) NATO Commander General Wesley Clark, the Pentagon's military road-map consisted of a sequence of countries: "[The] five-year campaign plan [includes]... a total of seven countries, beginning with Iraq, then Syria, Lebanon, Libya, Iran, Somalia and Sudan.":

As I [Wesley Clark] went back through the Pentagon in November 2001, one of the senior military staff officers had time for a chat. Yes, we were still on track for going against Iraq, he said. But there was more. This was being discussed as part of a five-year campaign plan, he said, and there were a total of seven countries, beginning with Iraq, then Syria, Lebanon, Libya, Iran, Somalia and Sudan.[8]

Simulated Scenarios of a Global War: The Vigilant Shield 07 War Games

In September 2006, the US conducted a scenario of all-out war directed against Iran. In contrast to TIRANNT, the Vigilant Shield 07 war games were not limited to a single Middle East war theater (e.g. Iran), they also include Russia, China and North Korea.

These war games conducted during Bush's second term were a dress rehearsal for the formulation of the Obama Administration's

The Vigilant Shield 07 War Games. Details and Sequencing: Simulating a War with Irmingham, Ruebeck, Churya, Nemazee (Iran, Russia, China, North Korea)

- Road to Conflict (RTC): 11 Sep – 15 Oct 06

  – Initial Irmingham Enrichment I&W [indications and warning] – Initial Ruebeki & Irmingham Involvement – Ruebek I&W, PACFLT [U.S. Pacific Fleet] Sub Deployments – Initial Nemazee ICBM [intercontinental ballistic missile] I&W – Initial MHLD [homeland defense?] I&W – Strategic IO [information operations (cyber warfare)] operations (Ruebek & Churya) – Ruebek & Irmingham Conduct Joint AD [air defense] Exercise

- Phase 1 / Deployment: 4 – 8 Dec 06

  – Rogue LRA [Ruebek long-range aviation] w/CALCM [conventional air launched cruise missile] Launch – Continue Monitoring Strategic Situation – Continue Monitoring Nemazee Situation

- Possible Nuclear Testing

- Probable ICBM Preparation

  – Continue Monitoring MHLD Situation

- Five VOIs [vessels of interest]

- Churya Flagged VOI into Dutch Harbor Supports BMDS [ballistic missile defense system] Threat to Ft Greely

  – Continue Monitoring IO Activities

  – Nemazee Conducts SLV [space launch vehicle] Launch

  – 8 Dec 06

- Phase 2 Minus 42 Days:

- Additional Nemazee ICBM Shipments to Launch Facilities

- RMOB [Russian main operating bases] Acft Conduct LR Navigation Flights

  – AS-15 [nuclear armed cruise missile] Handling at RMOBs

  – Minus 41 Days:

- Additional Nemazee ICBM Preps at Launch Pad # 2

  – Minus 40 Days:

- Activity at Nemazee Nuclear Test Facilities
- Minus 35 Days:
- DOS [Department of State] Travel Warning
- Minus 30 Days:
- Ruebek LRA Deploys Acft to Anadyr & Vorkuta
- Phase 2 Minus 30 Days:
- Growing International Condemnation of Ruebek
- Ruebek Deploys Submarines
- Minus 20 Days:
- Nemazee Recalls Reservists
- Minus 14 Days:
- DOS Draw-down Sequencing
- Minus 13 Days:
- Ruebek Closes US Embassy in Washington DC
- Minus 11 Days:
- Nemazee Conducts Fueling of Additional ICBMs
- Ruebeki Presidential Statement on Possible US Attack
- Phase 2 Minus 10 Days:
- POTUS Addresses Congress on War Powers Act
- Minus 6 Days:
- Ruebek President Calls "Situation Grave"
- Minus 5 Days:
- CALCM Activity at Anadyr, Vorkuta, and Tiksi
- Ruebeki SS-25 [nuclear armed mobile ICBMs] Conduct out of Garrison Deployments • Nemazee Assembling ICBM for Probable Launch
- Minus 4 Days: • Ruebek Closes US Embassy in Washington DC
- Ruebek Acft Conduct Outer ADIZ [air defense identification zone] Pentrations
- Mid-Air Collison w/NORAD Acft During ADIZ Penetration
- Phase 2 Minus 4 Days:

The Vigilant Shield 07 War Games... (cont.)

• Nemazee ICBM Launch Azimuth Threatens US

– Minus 3 Days:

• NATO Diplomatic Efforts Fail to Diffuse Crisis • USAMB to Ruebek Recalled for Consultation

• POTUS Addresses Nation

– Minus 2 Days:

• Nemazee Leadership Movement

– Minus 1 Day: • Ruebek Expels US Mission

• Phase 2 / Execution: 10 – 14 Dec 06

– Pre-Attack I & W – Imminent Terrorist Attack on Pentagon Suggests Pentagon COOP [continuity of operations plan]

– Nemazee Conducts 2 x ICBM Combat Launches Against United States

– Ruebek Conducts Limited Strategic Attack on United States

• Wave 1 – 8 x Bear H Defense Suppression w/CALCM

• Wave 2 – Limited ICBM & SLBM Attack – 2 x ICBM Launched (1 impacts CMOC [Cheyenne Mountain], 1 malfunctions) – 2 x SLBM Launched Pierside (1 impacts SITE-R ["Raven Rock" bunker on the Maryland-Pennsylvania border], 1 malfunctions) – 3 x Bear H from Dispersal Bases w/ALCM (Eielson AFB, CANR, Cold Lake) – US Conducts Limited Retaliatory Attack on Ruebek • 1 x ICBM C2 Facility • 1 x ICBM Against ICBM Launch Location

• Phase 2 / Execution: – Ruebek Prepares Additional Attack on United States

• Wave 3 – Prepares for Additional Strategic Attacks – 1 x ICBM Movement, NO Launch – 3 x SLBM PACFLT Pierside Missile Handling Activity (NO Launch) – 6 x BEAR H (launch & RTB [return to base]) w/6 x ALCM (NO launch)"

Source: William Arkin, *The Vigilant Shield 07 War Games: Scenario opposing the US to Russia, China, Iran and North Korea, Washington Post Blog,* October 6, 2006, *http://www.global research.ca/index.php?context=va&aid=4730.* Author's note: The above text of Vigilant Shield 07 is verbatim.

Iran policy, characterized by threats directed against Tehran regarding its nuclear enrichment program, as well as veiled threats directed against China, Russia and North Korea. These simulations of an attack on Iran have a direct bearing on US-NATO war preparations.

The details of the Vigilant Shield 07 exercise scenario, is contained in a US Northern Command (NORTHCOM) briefing dated August 2006, leaked to the Washington Post.[9]

The enemies in this simulation are Irmingham [Iran], Nemazee [North Korea], Ruebek [Russia], Churya [China].

The Role of Israel

There has been much debate regarding the role of Israel in initiating an attack against Iran. Israel is part of a military alliance. Tel Aviv is not a prime mover. It does not have a separate and distinct military agenda. Israel is integrated into the "war plan for major combat operations" against Iran formulated in 2006 by US Strategic Command (USSTRATCOM).

In the context of large scale military operations, an uncoordinated unilateral military action by one coalition partner, namely Israel, is an impossibility from a military and strategic standpoint. Israel is a *de facto* member of NATO. Any action by Israel would require a "green light" from Washington. An attack by Israel could, however, be used as a "trigger mechanism" which would unleash an all-out war against Iran, as well as retaliation by Iran directed against Israel.

In this regard, there are indications that Washington had indeed envisaged the option of an initial (US-backed) attack by Israel rather than an outright US-led military operation directed against Iran. In this context, the Israeli attack – although led in close liaison with the Pentagon and NATO – would be presented to public opinion as a unilateral decision by Tel Aviv. It would then be used by Washington to justify, in the eyes of world opinion, a military intervention of the US and NATO with a view to "defending Israel", rather than attacking Iran. Under existing military cooperation agreements, both the US and NATO would be "obligated" to "defend Israel" against Iran and Syria.

Cheney: "Israel Might Do it Without Being Asked"

At the outset of Bush's second term, (former) Vice President Dick Cheney hinted, in no uncertain terms, that Iran was "right at the top of the list" of the "rogue enemies" of America, and that Israel would, so to speak, "be doing the bombing for us", without US military involvement and without us putting pressure on them "to do it".[10] According to Cheney:

> One of the concerns people have is that Israel might do it without being asked... Given the fact that Iran has a stated policy that their objective is the destruction of Israel, the Israelis might well decide to act first, and let the rest of the world worry about cleaning up the diplomatic mess afterwards.[11]

Commenting on the Vice President's assertion, former National Security adviser Zbigniew Brzezinski, confirmed with some apprehension, yes: Cheney wants Prime Minister Ariel Sharon to act on America's behalf and "do it" for us:

> Iran I think is more ambiguous. And there the issue is certainly not tyranny; it's nuclear weapons. And the vice president today in a kind of a strange parallel statement to this declaration of freedom hinted that the Israelis may do it and in fact used language which sounds like a justification or even an encouragement for the Israelis to do it.[12]

US Israel Military Coordination

What we are dealing with is a joint US-NATO-Israel military operation to bomb Iran, which has been in the active planning stage since 2004. Officials in the Defense Department, under Bush and Obama, have been working assiduously with their Israeli military and intelligence counterparts, carefully identifying targets inside Iran. In practical military terms, any action by Israel would have to be planned and coordinated at the highest levels of the US-led coalition.

An attack by Israel would also require coordinated US-NATO logistical support, particularly with regard to Israel's air defense system, which since January 2009 is fully integrated into that of the US and NATO.[13] Israel's X band radar system established in early 2009 with US technical support has "integrate[d] Israel's missile defenses with the U.S. global missile [Space-based] detection network, which includes satellites, Aegis ships on the Mediterranean, Persian Gulf and Red Sea, and land-based Patriot radars and interceptors."[14] What this means is that Washington ultimately calls the shots.

The US, rather than Israel, controls the air defense system: "'This is and will remain a U.S. radar system,' Pentagon spokesman Geoff Morrell said. 'So this is not something we are giving or selling to the Israelis and it is something that will likely require U.S. personnel on-site to operate.'"[15]

Israel's Nuclear Weapons

Today, estimates of the Israeli nuclear arsenal range from a minimum of 200 to a maximum of about 500. Whatever the number, there is little doubt that Israeli nukes are among the world's most sophisticated, largely designed for "war fighting" in the Middle East. A staple of the Israeli nuclear arsenal are "neutron bombs," miniaturized thermonuclear bombs designed to maximize deadly gamma radiation while minimizing blast effects and long term radiation – in essence designed to kill people while leaving property intact.[17]

In 1986, an Israeli civil servant who worked in the state-owned nuclear industry flew to London where he was invited to meet with reporters working for *The Sunday Times*. In these press briefings, Mordechai Vanunu revealed Israel's top secret – the Israelis had gained control of a growing stockpile of nuclear warheads.[18]

According to *Jane's Defense Weekly* Israel has between 100 and 300 nuclear warheads, most of them are probably being kept in unassembled mode but can become fully functional "in a matter of days".[19]

Based on plausible upper and lower bounds of the operating practices at the reactor, Israel could have thus produced enough plutonium for at least 100 nuclear weapons, but probably not significantly more than 200 weapons.[20]

[Israel possesses] more than 100 weapons, mainly two-stage thermonuclear devices, capable of being delivered by missile, fighter-bomber, or submarine.[21]

The US military oversees Israel's Air Defense system, which is integrated into the Pentagon's global system. In other words, Israel cannot launch a war against Iran without Washington's consent. Hence the importance of the so-called "Green Light" legislation in the US Congress sponsored by the Republican party under House Resolution 1553, which explicitly supports an Israeli attack on Iran:

> The measure, introduced by Texas Republican Louie Gohmert and 46 of his colleagues, endorses Israel's use of "all means necessary" against Iran "including the use of military force... We've got to get this done. We need to show our support for Israel. We need to quit playing games with this critical ally in such a difficult area."[16]

In practice, the proposed legislation was a "green light" to the White House and the Pentagon rather than to Israel. It constitutes a rubber stamp to a US-sponsored war on Iran which uses Israel as a convenient military launch pad. It also serves as a justification to wage war with a view to defending Israel.

In this context, Israel could indeed provide the pretext to wage war, in response to alleged Hamas or Hezbollah attacks and/or the triggering of hostilities on the border of Israel with Lebanon. What is crucial to understand is that a minor "incident" could be used as a pretext to spark off a major military operation against Iran.

Known to US military planners, Israel (rather than the USA) would be the first target of military retaliation by Iran. Broadly speaking, Israelis would be the victims of the machinations of both Washington and their own government. It is, in this regard, absolutely crucial that Israelis forcefully oppose any action by the Netanyahu government to attack Iran.

Tactical Nuclear Weapons directed against Iran

Confirmed by military documents as well as official statements, both the US and Israel contemplate the use of nuclear weapons directed against Iran. In 2006, US Strategic Command (USSTRAT-COM) announced it had achieved an operational capability for rapidly striking targets around the globe using nuclear or conven-

Using Fake Intelligence to Justify a Pre-emptive Nuclear War on Iran

In November 2005, *The New York Times* published a report by William J. Broad and David E. Sanger entitled "Relying on Computer, U.S. Seeks to Prove Iran's Nuclear Aims".[22]

Washington's allegations, reported in the NYT hinged upon documents "obtained from a stolen Iranian computer by an unknown source and given to US intelligence in 2004."[23]

These documents included "a series of drawings of a missile re-entry vehicle" which allegedly could accommodate an Iranian produced nuclear weapon:

> In mid-July, senior American intelligence officials called the leaders of the international atomic inspection agency to the top of a skyscraper overlooking the Danube in Vienna and unveiled the contents of what they said was a stolen Iranian laptop computer.
>
> The Americans flashed on a screen and spread over a conference table selections from more than a thousand pages of Iranian computer simulations and accounts of experiments, saying they showed a long effort to design a nuclear warhead...
>
> The documents, the Americans acknowledged from the start, do not prove that Iran has an atomic bomb. They presented them as the strongest evidence yet that, despite Iran's insistence that its nuclear program is peaceful, the country is trying to *develop a compact warhead to fit atop its Shahab missile*, which can reach Israel and other countries in the Middle East.[24]

These "secret documents" were subsequently submitted by the US State Department to the International Atomic Energy Agency (IAEA), with a view to demonstrating that Iran was developing a nuclear weapons program.

While their authenticity has been questioned on several occasions, an article by Gareth Porter confirms unequivocally that the mysterious laptop documents are fake. The drawings contained in the documents do not pertain to the Shahab missile but to an obsolete North Korean missile system which was decommissioned by Iran in the mid-1990s. The drawings presented by US State Department officials pertained to the "Wrong Missile Warhead":

> In July 2005... Robert Joseph, US undersecretary of state for arms control and international security, made a formal presentation on the purported Iranian nuclear weapons program documents to the agency's leading officials in Vienna. Joseph flashed excerpts from the documents on the screen, giving special attention to the series of technical drawings or "schematics" showing 18 different ways of fitting an unidentified payload into the re-entry vehicle or "warhead" of Iran's medium-range ballistic missile, the Shahab-3.
>
> When IAEA analysts were allowed to study the documents, however, they discovered that those schematics were based on a re-entry vehicle that the analysts knew had already been abandoned by the Iranian military in favor of a new, improved design. The warhead shown in the schematics *had the familiar "dunce cap" shape of the original North Korean No Dong missile, which Iran had acquired in the mid-1990s...*
>
> The laptop documents had depicted the wrong re-entry vehicle being redesigned.[25]

Who was behind the production of fake intelligence? Gareth Porter suggests that Israel's Mossad could have been a source of fake intelligence:

> The origin of the laptop documents may never be proven conclusively, but the accumulated evidence points to Israel as the source. As early as 1995, the head of the Israel Defense Forces' military intelligence research and assessment division, Yaakov Amidror, tried unsuccessfully to persuade his American counterparts that Iran was planning to "go nuclear." By 2003-2004, Mossad's reporting on the Iranian nuclear program was viewed by high-ranking CIA officials as an effort to pressure the Bush administration into considering military action against Iran's nuclear sites, according to Israeli sources cited by a pro-Israeli news service.[26]

The laptop documents were essential to sustaining Washington's position in favor of sanctions in the UN Security Council.[27]

tional weapons. This announcement was made after the conduct of military simulations pertaining to a US-led nuclear attack against a fictional country.[28]

Continuity in relation to the Bush-Cheney era: President Obama has largely endorsed the doctrine of pre-emptive use of nuclear weapons formulated by the previous administration. Under the 2010 Nuclear Posture Review, the Obama administration confirmed "that it is reserving the right to use nuclear weapons against Iran" for its non-compliance with US demands regarding its alleged (nonexistent) nuclear weapons program.[29] The Obama administration has also intimated that it would use nukes in the case of an Iranian response to an Israeli attack on Iran.[30] Israel has also drawn up its own "secret plans" to bomb Iran with tactical nuclear weapons:

> Israeli military commanders believe conventional strikes may no longer be enough to annihilate increasingly well-defended enrichment facilities. Several have been built beneath at least 70ft of concrete and rock. However, the nuclear-tipped bunker-busters would be used only if a conventional attack was ruled out and if the United States declined to intervene, senior sources said.[31]

Obama's statements on the use of nuclear weapons against Iran and North Korea are consistent with post-9/11 US nuclear weapons doctrine, which allows for the use of tactical nuclear weapons in the conventional war theater.

Through a propaganda campaign which has enlisted the support of "authoritative" nuclear scientists, mini-nukes are upheld as an instrument of peace, namely a means of combating "Islamic terrorism" and instating Western style "democracy" in Iran. The low-yield nukes have been cleared for "battlefield use". They are slated to be used against Iran and Syria in the next stage of America's "War on Terrorism" alongside conventional weapons.

> Administration officials argue that low-yield nuclear weapons are needed as a credible deterrent against rogue states [Iran, Syria, North Korea]. Their logic is that existing nuclear

weapons are too destructive to be used except in a full-scale nuclear war. Potential enemies realize this, thus they do not consider the threat of nuclear retaliation to be credible. However, low-yield nuclear weapons are less destructive, thus might conceivably be used. That would make them more effective as a deterrent.[32]

The preferred nuclear weapon to be used against Iran are tactical nuclear weapons (Made in America), namely bunker buster bombs with nuclear warheads (e.g. B61.11), with an explosive capacity between one third to six times a Hiroshima bomb. The B61-11 is the "nuclear version" of the "conventional" BLU 113 or Guided Bomb Unit GBU-28. It can be delivered in much same way as the conventional bunker buster bomb.[33] While the US does not contemplate the use of strategic nuclear weapons against Iran, Israel's nuclear arsenal is largely composed of similar thermonuclear bombs which are deployed and could be used in a war with Iran. Under Israel's Jericho III missile system, with a range between 4,800 km to 6,500 km, all Iran would be within reach.

Radioactive Fallout

The issue of radioactive fallout and contamination, while casually dismissed by US-NATO military analysts, would be devastating, potentially affecting a large part of the Middle East (including Israel) and Central Asia. In an utterly twisted logic, nuclear weapons are presented as a means to building peace and preventing "collateral damage". Iran's nonexistent nuclear weapons are a threat to global security, whereas those of the US and Israel are "instruments of peace", "harmless to the surrounding civilian population".

"The Mother of All Bombs" (MOAB) Slated to be Used Against Iran

Of military significance within the US conventional weapons arsenal is the 21,500-pound "monster weapon" nicknamed the "mother of all bombs". The GBU-43/B or Massive Ordnance Air Blast bomb (MOAB) was categorized "as the most powerful non-nu-

History of the B61 Thermonuclear Bomb

The B-61 thermonuclear bomb, first produced in 1966, is described as a light weight nuclear device. Its construction essentially extends the technology of the older version of tactical nuclear warheads.[34]

The B61-11 earth-penetrating version of the B61 was developed in the immediate wake of the Cold War under the Clinton administration. It was configured initially to have a "low" 10 kiloton yield, 66.6 percent of a Hiroshima bomb, for (post-Cold War) battlefield operations:

> In October 1993, Harold Smith, Assistant to the Secretary of Defense for Atomic Energy, sought approval to develop an alternative to the B53 high-yield nuclear bomb, which was the principal "bunker buster" weapon in the U.S. arsenal. Under the guise of "weapons modernization," Smith was pushing the development of the B61-Mod 11... [which] was developed and put into the stockpile without full-scale nuclear tests. Some critics have maintained that the B61-11 is a new nuclear weapon, but the US has said all along that the B61-11 is not new, but a modification of older B61s to give the weapon an earth-penetrating capability to destroy buried targets.[35]

The B61-11 was intended for the Middle East. The Clinton administration had in fact threatened to use it against Libya, suggesting that Libya's alleged underground chemical weapons facility at Tarhunah "might be a target of the then-newly deployed B61-11 earth-penetrating nuclear weapon."[36]

Military documents distinguish between the NEP and the "mini-nuke" which are nuclear weapons with a yield of less than 10 kilotons (two-thirds of a Hiroshima bomb). The NEP can have a yield of up to a thousand kilotons, or seventy times a Hiroshima bomb. This distinction between mini-nukes and NEPs is in many regards misleading. In practice there is no dividing line. We are broadly dealing with the same type of weaponry: the B61-11 has several "available yields", ranging from "low yields" of less than one kiloton, to mid-range and up to the 1000 kiloton bomb. In all cases, the radioactive fallout is devastating. Moreover, the B61 series of thermonuclear weapons includes several models with distinct specifications: the B61-11, the B61-3, B61-4, B61-7 and B61-10. Each of these bombs has several "available yields". What is contemplated for theater use is the "low yield" 10 kt bomb, two-thirds of a Hiroshima bomb.

clear weapon ever designed" with the largest yield in the US conventional arsenal.[38]

The MOAB was tested in early March 2003 before being deployed to the Iraq war theater. According to US military sources, the Joint Chiefs of Staff had advised the government of Saddam Hussein prior to launching the 2003 war that the "mother of all bombs" was to be used against Iraq. (There were unconfirmed reports that it had been used in Iraq.)

The U.S. Department of Defense has confirmed that it intends to use the "Mother of All Bombs" (MOAB) against Iran. The MOAB is said to be "ideally suited to hit deeply buried nuclear facilities such as Natanz or Qom in Iran"[39] The truth of the matter is that the MOAB, given its explosive capacity, would result in extremely large civilian casualties. It is a conventional "killing machine" with a nuclear-type mushroom cloud.

The procurement of four MOABs was commissioned in October 2009 at the hefty cost of $58.4 million, ($14.6 million for each bomb). This amount included the costs of development and testing as well as integration of the MOAB bombs onto B-2 stealth bombers.[40] This procurement is directly linked to war preparations in relation to Iran. The notification was contained in a 93-page "reprogramming memo" which included the following instructions:

> "The Department has an Urgent Operational Need (UON) for the capability to strike hard and deeply buried targets in high threat environments. The MOP [Mother of All Bombs] is the weapon of choice to meet the requirements of the UON [Urgent Operational Need]." It further states that the request is endorsed by Pacific Command (which has responsibility over North Korea) and Central Command (which has responsibility over Iran).[41]

Extensive Destruction of Iran's Infrastructure

The Pentagon is planning on a process of extensive destruction of Iran's infrastructure and mass civilian casualties through the combined use of tactical nukes and monster conventional mushroom cloud bombs, including the MOAB and the larger GBU-57A/B or

Nuclear Winter

According to nuclear scientist Alan Rock:

The direct effects of the nuclear weapons, blast, radioactivity, fires and extensive pollution, would kill millions of people, but only those near the targets. However, the fires would have another effect. The massive amounts of dark smoke from the fires would be lofted into the upper troposphere, 10-15 kilometers (6-9 miles) above the Earth's surface, and then absorption of sunlight would further heat the smoke, lifting it into the stratosphere, a layer where the smoke would persist for years, with no rain to wash it out.

The climatic effects of smoke from fires started by nuclear war depend on the amount of smoke. Our new calculations show that for fifty nuclear weapons dropped on two countries, on the targets that would produce the maximum amount of smoke, about five megatons (Tg) of black smoke would be produced, accounting for the amount emitted from the fires and the amount immediately washed out in rain. As the smoke is lofted into the stratosphere, it would be transported around the world by the prevailing winds.

Compared to climate change for the past millennium, even the five Tg case (a war between India and Pakistan) would plunge the planet into temperatures colder than the Little Ice Age (approximately 1600-1850). This would be essentially instantly, and agriculture would be severely threatened. Larger amounts of smoke would produce larger climate changes, and for the 150 Tg case produce a true nuclear winter, making agriculture impossible for years. In both cases, new climate model simulations show that the effects would last for more than a decade.

Models made by Russian and American scientists showed that a nuclear war would result in a nuclear winter that would be extremely destructive to all life on Earth; the knowledge of that was a great stimulus to us, to people of honor and morality, to act in that situation.

Since the 1980s, the number of nuclear weapons in the world has decreased to 1/3 of the peak number of more than 70,000. The consequences of regional-scale nuclear conflicts are unexpectedly large, with the potential to become global catastrophes... The current and projected American and Russian nuclear arsenals can still produce nuclear winter. Only nuclear disarmament will prevent the possibility of a nuclear environmental catastrophe.[37]

Massive Ordnance Penetrator (MOP), which surpasses the MOAB in terms of explosive capacity. The MOP is described as "a powerful new bomb aimed squarely at the underground nuclear facilities of Iran and North Korea. The gargantuan bomb – longer than 11 persons standing shoulder-to-shoulder or more than 20 feet base to nose."[42]

These are WMDs in the true sense of the word. The not-so-hidden objective of the MOAB and MOP, including the American nickname used to casually describe the MOAB ("mother of all bombs"), is mass destruction and mass civilian casualties with a view to instilling fear and despair.

State of the Art Weaponry: "War Made Possible Through New Technologies"

The process of US military decision-making in relation to Iran is supported by "Star Wars", the militarization of outer space and the revolution in communications and information systems. Given the advances in military technology and the development of new weapons systems, an attack on Iran would be significantly different in terms of the mix of weapons systems, when compared to the March 2003 *Blitzkrieg* launched against Iraq. The Iran operation is slated to use the most advanced weapons systems in support of its aerial attacks. In all likelihood, new weapons systems will be tested.

The 2000 Project of the New American Century (PNAC) document entitled *Rebuilding American Defenses*, outlined the mandate of the US military in terms of large scale theater wars, to be waged simultaneously in different regions of the world:

> *"Fight and decisively win multiple, simultaneous major theater wars."*

This formulation is tantamount to a global war of conquest by a single imperial superpower. The PNAC document also called for the transformation of US forces to exploit the "revolution in military affairs", namely the implementation of "war made possible through new technologies."[43] The latter consists in developing and perfecting a state of the art *global killing machine* based on an arsenal of sophisticated new weaponry, which would eventually replace the "current paradigms of warfare":

> Thus, it can be foreseen that the process of transformation will in fact be a two-stage process: *first of transition, then of more thoroughgoing transformation. The breakpoint will come when a preponderance of new weapons systems begins to enter service,* perhaps when, for example, unmanned aerial vehicles begin to be as numerous as manned aircraft. In this regard, the Pentagon should be very wary of making large investments in new programs—tanks, planes, aircraft carriers, for example—that would commit U.S. forces to current paradigms of warfare for many decades to come.[44]

The war on Iran could indeed mark this crucial breakpoint, with new space-based weapons systems being applied with a view to disabling an enemy which has significant conventional military capabilities including more than half a million ground forces.

Electromagnetic Weapons

Electromagnetic weapons could be used to destabilize Iran's communications systems, disable electric power generation, undermine and destabilize command and control, government infrastructure, transportation, energy, etc. Within the same family of weapons, environmental modifications techniques (ENMOD) (weather warfare) developed under the HAARP program could also be applied.[45] These weapons systems are fully operational. In this context, the US Air Force document AF 2025 explicitly acknowledged the military applications of weather modification technologies:

> Weather modification will become a part of domestic and international security and could be done unilaterally... It could have offensive and defensive applications and even be used for deterrence purposes. The ability to generate precipitation, fog, and storms on earth or to modify space weather, improve communications through ionospheric modification (the use of ionospheric mirrors), and the production of artificial weather

all are a part of an integrated set of technologies which can provide substantial increase in US, or degraded capability in an adversary, to achieve global awareness, reach, and power.[46]

Electromagnetic radiation enabling "remote health impairment" might also be envisaged in the war theater.[47] In turn, new uses of biological weapons by the US military might also be envisaged as suggested by the PNAC: "Advanced forms of biological warfare that can "target" specific genotypes may transform biological warfare from the realm of terror to a politically useful tool."[48]

Iran's Military Capabilities: Medium and Long Range Missiles

Iran has advanced military capabilities, including medium and long range missiles capable of reaching targets in Israel and the Gulf States. Hence the emphasis by the US-NATO Israel alliance on the use of nuclear weapons, which are slated to be used either pre-emptively or in response to an Iranian retaliatory missile attack.

In November 2006, Iran's tests of its surface missiles were marked by precise planning in a carefully staged operation. According to a senior American missile expert (quoted by *Debka*), "the Iranians demonstrated up-to-date missile-launching technology which the West had not known them to possess."[49] Israel acknowledged that "the Shehab-3, [with a] 2,000-km range brings Israel, the Middle East and Europe within reach."[50]

According to Uzi Rubin, former head of Israel's anti-ballistic missile program, "the intensity of the military exercise was unprecedented... It was meant to make an impression – and it made an impression."[51]

The 2006 exercises, while creating a political stir in the US and Israel, did not in any way modify US-NATO-Israeli resolve to wage on Iran.

Tehran has confirmed in several statements that it will respond if attacked. Israel would be the immediate object of Iranian missile attacks as confirmed by the Iranian government.

The issue of Israel's air defense system is therefore crucial. US and allied military facilities in the Gulf States, Turkey, Saudi Arabia, Afghanistan and Iraq could also be targeted by Iran.

Iran's Ground Forces

While Iran is encircled by US and allied military bases, the Islamic Republic has significant military capabilities. What is important to acknowledge is the sheer size of Iranian forces in terms of personnel (army, navy, air force) when compared to US and NATO forces serving in Afghanistan and Iraq. Confronted with a well organized insurgency, coalition forces are already overstretched in both Afghanistan and Iraq. Would these forces be able to cope if Iranian ground forces were to enter the existing battlefield in Iraq and Afghanistan?

The potential of the national resistance movements in both Afghanistan and Iraq to US and allied occupation would inevitably be enhanced.

Iranian ground forces are of the order of 700,000 of which 130,000 are professional soldiers, 220,000 are conscripts and 350,000 are reservists. There are 18,000 personnel in Iran's Navy and 52,000 in the air force.[52] According to the International Institute for Strategic Studies, "the Revolutionary Guards has an estimated 125,000 personnel in five branches: its own Navy, Air Force and Ground Forces; and the Quds Force (Special Forces)." According to the CISS, Iran's Basij paramilitary volunteer force controlled by the Revolutionary Guards "has an estimated 90,000 active-duty full-time uniformed members, 300,000 reservists, and a total of 11 million men that can be mobilized if need be."[53] In other words, Iran can mobilize up to half a million regular troops and several million militia. Its Quds special forces are already operating inside Iraq.

US Military and Allied Facilities Surrounding Iran

For several years now, Iran has been conducting its own war drills and exercises. While its air force has weaknesses, its intermediate and long-range missiles are fully operational. Iran's military is in a state of readiness. Iranian troop concentrations are currently within a few kilometers of the Iraqi and Afghan borders, and within proximity of Kuwait. The Iranian Navy is deployed in the Persian Gulf within proximity of US and allied military facilities in the United Arab Emirates.

It is worth noting that in response to Iran's military build-up, the US has been transferring large amounts of weapons to its non-NATO allies in the Persian Gulf including Kuwait and Saudi Arabia.

While Iran's advanced weapons do not measure up to those of the US and NATO, Iranian forces would be in a position to inflict substantial losses to coalition forces in a conventional war theater, on the ground in Iraq and Afghanistan. Iranian ground troops and tanks in December 2009 crossed the border into Iraq without being confronted or challenged by allied forces and occupied a disputed territory in the East Maysan oil field.

Even in the event of an effective *Blitzkrieg*, which targets Iran's military facilities, its communications systems, etc., through massive aerial bombing, using cruise missiles, conventional bunker buster bombs and tactical nuclear weapons, a war with Iran, once initiated, could eventually lead into a ground war. This is something which US military planners have no doubt contemplated in their simulated war scenarios. An operation of this nature would result in significant military and civilian casualties, particularly if nuclear weapons are used.

The expanded budget for the war in Afghanistan approved by the US Congress is also intended to be used in the eventuality of an attack on Iran. Within a scenario of escalation, Iranian troops could cross the border into Iraq and Afghanistan. In turn, military escalation using nuclear weapons could lead us into a World War III scenario, extending beyond the Middle East Central Asian region. In a very real sense, this military project, which has been on the Pentagon's drawing board for more than five years, threatens the future of humanity.

Our focus in this essay has been on war preparations. The fact that war preparations are in an advanced state of readiness does not imply that these war plans will be carried out. The US-NATO-Israel alliance realizes that the enemy has significant capabilities to respond and retaliate. This factor in itself has been crucial over the last five years in the decision by the US and its allies to postpone an attack on Iran.

Another crucial factor is the structure of military alliances. Whereas NATO has become a formidable force, the Shanghai Cooperation Organization (SCO), which constitutes an alliance between Russia and China and several former Soviet republics has been significantly weakened. The ongoing US military threats directed against China and Russia are intended to weaken the SCO and discourage any form of military action on the part of Iran's allies in the case of a US-NATO-Israeli attack.

NOTES

1. Globalsecurity.org, "Target Iran: Air Strikes", http://www.globalsecurity.org/mili tary/ops/iran-strikes.htm.

2. US Department of Defense, 2006 Quadrennial Defense Review, http://www.de fense.gov/qdr/report/Report20060203.pdf, Washington DC, 2006.

3. William Arkin, *Washington Post,* 16 April 2006.

4. *Ibid.*

5. *The New Statesman,* 19 February 2007.

6. Philip Giraldi, "Deep Background", op. cit., *The American Conservative,* http://www.amconmag.com/article/2005/aug/01/00027//, August 2005.

7. United States Central Command (USCENTCOM), http://www.milnet.com/milnet/ pentagon/centcom/chap1/stratgic.htm#USPolicy, link no longer active, archived at http://tinyurl.com/37gafu9.

8. Wesley Clark, *Winning Modern Wars: Iraq, Terrorism, and the American Empire,* p. 130, New York, PublicAffairs, 2004. Also quoted in "Secret 2001 Pentagon Plan to Attack Lebanon", *Global Research,* http://www.globalresearch.ca/index.php?con text=va&aid=2797, 23 July 2006. See also Sydney H. Schanberg, "The Secrets Clark Kept What the General Never Told Us About the Bush Plan for Serial War", *The Village Voice,* http://www.villagevoice.com/2003-09-30/news/thesecrets-clark-kept/, 30 September 2003.

9. William M. Arkin, "The Vigilant Shield 07 War Games: Scenario opposing the US to Russia, China, Iran and North Korea", *Washington Post Blog,* http://blog.washington post.com/earlywarning/war_games/, 6 October 2006.

10. Michel Chossudovsky, "Planned US-Israeli Attack on Iran", *Global Research,* http://www.globalresearch.ca/articles/CHO505A.html, 1 May 2005.

11. Dick Cheney, quoted from an MSNBC Interview, 20 January 2005.

12. Zbigniew Brzezinski, "Analysts Discuss the Theme of Democracy in President Bush's Inaugural Address", *PBS Online NewsHour,* http://www.pbs.org/newshour/bb/

white_house/jan-june05/democracy_1-20.html, January 20, 2005.

13. Michel Chossudovsky, "Unusually Large U.S. Weapons Shipment to Israel: Are the US and Israel Planning a Broader Middle East War?", *Global Research*, http://www.glob alresearch.ca/index.php?context=va&aid=11743, 11 January 2009.

14. *Defense Talk,* http://www.defencetalk.com/news/publish/defence, 6 January 2009.

15. *Israel National News,* 9 January 2009.

16. Webster Tarpley, "Fidel Castro Warns of Imminent Nuclear War; Admiral Mullen Threatens Iran; US-Israel vs. Iran-Hezbollah Confrontation Builds On", *Global Research,* http://globalresearch.ca/index.php?context=va&aid=20571, 10 August 2010.

17. John Steinbach, "Israeli Weapons of Mass Destruction: a Threat to Peace", *Global Research,* http://www.globalresearch.ca/articles/STE203A.html, 3 March 2002.

18. Michael Carmichael, "Israel's plans to Wage Nuclear War on Iran: History of Israel's Arsenal", *Global Research,* http://www.globalresearch.ca/index.php?context= va&aid=4477, 15 January 2007.

19. Ynet News, "Analysts: Israel viewed as world's 6th nuclear power", *Ynet News.com,* http://www.ynetnews.com/articles/0,7340,L-3873755,00.html, 10 April 2010.

20. Federation of American Scientists, "Nuclear Weapons – Israel", http://www. fas.org/nuke/guide/israel/nuke/, 8 January 2007.

21. Jeffrey Goldberg, "The Point of No Return", *The Atlantic,* http://www. theatlantic.com/magazine/print/2010/09/the-point-of-no-return/8186/, September 2010.

22. William J. Broad and David E. Sanger, "Relying on Computer, U.S. Seeks to Prove Iran's Nuclear Aims", *The New York Times,* http://www.nytimes.com/2005/11/13/inter national/middleeast/13nukes.html?_r=2&pagewanted=print, 13 November 2005.

23. Gareth Porter, "Exclusive Report: Evidence of Iran Nuclear Weapons Program May Be Fraudulent", *Global Research,* http://globalresearch.ca/index.php?context= va&aid=21994, 18 November 2010.

24. William J. Broad and David E. Sanger, "Relying on Computer, U.S. Seeks to Prove Iran's Nuclear Aims", *op. cit., The New York Times,* http://www.nytimes.com/ 2005/11/13/international/middleeast/13nukes.html?_r=2&pagewanted=print, 13 November 2005, italics added.

25. Gareth Porter, "Exclusive Report: Evidence of Iran Nuclear Weapons Program May Be Fraudulent", *op. cit., Global Research,* http://globalresearch.ca/index.php?con text=va&aid=21994, 18 November 2010

26. *Ibid.*

27. Michel Chossudovsky, "The Mysterious "Laptop Documents". Using Fake Intelligence to Justify a Pre-emptive Nuclear War on Iran", *Global Research,* http://global research.ca/index.php?context=va&aid=22085, 24 November 2010.

28. David Ruppe, "Preemptive Nuclear War in a State of Readiness: U.S. Command Declares Global Strike Capability", *Global Security Newswire,* http://www.nti.org/gsn/article/us-command-declares-global-strike-capability/, 2 December 2005.

29. Gareth Porter, "U.S. Nuclear Option on Iran Linked to Israeli Attack Threat", *IPS News.net,* http://ipsnews.net/news.asp?idnews=51172, 23 April 2010.

30. *Ibid.*

31. Uzi Mahnaimi and Sarah Baxter, "Revealed: Israel plans nuclear strike on Iran", *Times Online,* http://www.timesonline.co.uk/tol/news/world/article1290331.ece, 7 January 2007.

32. William Matthews, "Opponents Surprised By Elimination of Nuke Research Funds", *Defense News,* 29 November 2004.

33. Michel Chossudovsky, "Tactical Nuclear Weapons against Afghanistan?", *Global Research,* http://www.globalresearch.ca/articles/CHO112C.html, 5 December 2001.

34. For further details see "The B61 (Mk-61) Bomb", Nuclear Weapons Archive, http://nuclearweaponarchive.org/Usa/Weapons/B61.html.

35. GlobalSecurity.org, "Weapons of Mass Destruction (WMD): B61", *GlobalSecurity.org,* http://www.globalsecurity.org/wmd/systems/b61.htm.

36. *The Record,* Bergen County, New Jersey, 23 February 2003.

37. See also Alan Robock, "Nuclear Winter", *Encyclopaedia of the Earth,* http://www.eoearth.org/article/Nuclear_winter, January 2009.

38. Wikipedia, "GBU-43/B Massive Ordnance Air Blast bomb", *Wikipedia,* http://en.wikipedia.org/wiki/GBU-43/B_Massive_Ordnance_Air_Blast_bomb.

39. Jonathan Karl, "Is the U.S. Preparing to Bomb Iran?", *ABC News,* http://abcnews.go.com/Politics/us-preparing-bomb-iran/story?id=8765343, 9 October 2009.

40. *Ibid.*

41. *Ibid.,* italics added.

42. Edwin Black, "Super Bunker-Buster Bombs Fast-Tracked for Possible Use Against Iran and North Korea Nuclear Programs", Cutting Edge, http://www.thecuttingedgenews.com/index.php?article=11609, 21 September 2009. To consult the official "unclassified" reprogramming memo and procurement information pertaining to the MOAB, see http://abcnews.go.com/images/Politics/reprogramming_memo_091006.pdf.

43. PNAC, "Rebuilding America's Defenses", Project for the New American Century, Washington DC, http://www.newamericancentury.org/RebuildingAmericas-Defenses.pdf, September 2000.

44. *Ibid.,* italics added.

45. Michel Chossudovsky, "'Owning the Weather' for Military Use", *Global Research,*

http://www.globalresearch.ca/articles/CHO409F.html, 27 September 2004.

46. Lt Gen Jay W. Kelley, "Air Force 2025 Executive Summary", http://web.archive.org/web/19970429005352/www.au.af.mil/au/2025/monographs/ES/e-s.htm. See also US Air Force, "Weather as a Force Multiplier: Owning the Weather in 2025", http://csat.au.af.mil/2025/volume3/vol3ch15.pdf. See also "Weather as a Force Multiplier: Owning the Weather in 2025", Chapter 1, http://www.fas.org/spp/mili tary/docops/usaf/2025/v3c15/v3c15-1.htm.

47. Mojmir Babacek, "Electromagnetic and Informational Weapons", *Global Research,* http://www.globalresearch.ca/articles/BAB408B.html, 6 August 2004.

48. Project for the New American Century, *op. cit.,* p. 60.

49. Michel Chossudovsky, "Iran's 'Power of Deterrence'", *Global Research,* http://www.globalresearch.ca/index.php?context=va&aid=3713, 5 November 2006.

50. *Ibid.*

51. CNS News, www.cnsnews.com, 3 November 2006.

52. Wikipedia, "Islamic Republic of Iran Army", *Wikipedia,* http://en.wikipedia.org/wiki/Islamic_Republic_of_Iran_Army.

53. Wikipedia, "Armed Forces of the Islamic Republic of Iran", *Wikipedia,* http://en.wikipedia.org/wiki/Armed_Forces_of_the_Islamic_Republic_of_Iran.

Chapter VI
REVERSING THE TIDE
──────── OF WAR ────────

A good versus evil dichotomy prevails. The perpetrators of war are presented as the victims.

Public opinion is misled: "We must fight against evil in all its forms as a means to preserving the Western way of life."

When a US-sponsored nuclear war becomes an "instrument of peace", condoned and accepted by the world's institutions and the highest authority including the United Nations, there is no turning back: human society has indelibly been precipitated headlong onto the path of self-destruction.

What is required is a mass movement of people which forcefully challenges the legitimacy of war and the New World Order, a global people's movement which criminalizes war.

Antiwar protest does not question the legitimacy of those to whom the protest is addressed. Protest is accepted under Western-style "democracy" precisely because it accepts the established political order, while exerting pressure on political leaders to shift their policy stance. Protest serves the interests of the war criminals in high office, to whom the demands are directed. Ultimately what is at stake is the legitimacy of the political and military actors and the economic power structures, which control the formulation and direction of US foreign policy.

While the Obama Administration implements a "war on terrorism", the evidence (including mountains of official documents) amply confirms that successive US administrations have supported, abetted and harbored international terrorism. This fact, in itself, must be suppressed because if it ever trickles down to the broader public, the legitimacy of the so-called "war on terrorism" collapses like a deck of cards. And in the process, the legitimacy of the main actors behind this system would be threatened.

America's holy crusade against Islamic fundamentalism constitutes the very foundations of America's national security doctrine. How does one effectively break the war and police state agendas? Essentially by refuting the "war on terrorism".

Antiwar sentiment in itself will not reverse the tide of war. What is needed is to consistently challenge the legitimacy of the main political and military actors, reveal the true face of the American Empire and the underlying criminalization of foreign policy. Ultimately what is required is to question the Obama Administration's "right to rule".

Revealing the Lie

The greatest enemy of the US government is the truth.

Revealing the lies behind the US Administration and its allies constitutes the basis for undermining the legitimacy of the main political and military actors.

Even if a majority of the population is against the war, this in itself will not prevent the war from occurring. The propaganda campaign's objective is to sustain the lies which support the legitimacy of the main political and military actors. A necessary condition for bringing down the rulers is to weaken and eventually dismantle their propaganda campaign.

How best to achieve this objective? By fully uncovering the lies behind the "war on terrorism" and revealing the complicity of the US administration in the events of 9/11. This is a big hoax, it's the biggest lie in US history. The war pretext does not stick and the rulers should be removed. Moreover, it is important to show that "Enemy Number One" (Osama bin Laden) is fabricated.

The covert operations in support of terrorist organizations, including the history of Al Qaeda's links to the CIA since the Soviet Afghan war, must be fully revealed because they relate directly to the wave of terrorist attacks which have occurred since September 11, all of which are said to have links to Al Qaeda.

To reverse the tide, the spreading of information at all levels which counteracts the propaganda campaign is required.

The truth undermines and overshadows the lie.

Once this truth becomes fully understood, the legitimacy of the rulers will collapse like a deck of cards.

This is what has to be achieved. But we can only achieve it by effectively counteracting the official propaganda campaign. This initiative requires the spreading of information in an extensive grassroots network, with a view to weakening and ultimately disabling the administration's propaganda machine.

When the lies – including those concerning September 11 – are fully revealed and understood by everybody, the legitimacy of the US-NATO-Israel military agenda will be broken. While this will not necessarily result in a fundamental and significant "regime change" in the US, a new "anti-war consensus" will have emerged, which may eventually pave the way for a broader struggle against the New World Order and the American Empire's quest for global domination.

Protest accepts the legitimacy of the leaders to whom the protests are being addressed. One does not reverse the tide by asking President Barack Obama, "please abide by the Geneva Convention and the Nuremberg Charter." Ultimately, a consistent antiwar agenda requires unseating the war criminals in high office as a first step towards disarming the institutions and corporate structures of the New World Order.

To break the Inquisition, we must also break its propaganda, its fear and intimidation campaign, which galvanize public opinion into accepting the "war on terrorism".

The Existing Anti-War Movement

The existing antiwar movement has since 2003 been substantially weakened and divided. It does not at present have the required organizational capabilities to wage this campaign. The antiwar movement is misinformed on the nature of the US military agenda. Several non-governmental organizations have placed the blame on Iran, for not complying with the "reasonable demands" of the "international community". These same organizations, which are committed to world peace, tend to downplay the implications of the proposed US bombing of Iran.

An important segment of the antiwar movement, including prominent "progressive" intellectuals, is tacitly supportive of the "war on terrorism". Al Qaeda is considered a threat: "we are against the war but we support the campaign against terrorism".

The 9/11 Truth Movement, which challenges US military doctrine and the pretext for waging war, is categorized by segments of the anti-war movement as "conspiracy theorists".

While we should build upon existing antiwar structures, a meaningful mass movement would require entirely different premises and strategies.

Manufacturing Dissent

The antiwar collectives in the US, Canada and Western Europe are composed of numerous trade unions, NGOs, community groups, etc., many of which are dependent on foundation and/or government funding. Several of these NGOs rely heavily on both public as well as private funding agencies including the Ford, Rockefeller and Mc-Carthy foundations, among others. While the anti-globalization and antiwar movements are opposed to Wall Street, the Big Five Defense Contractors (i.e. weapons producers) and the Texas oil giants controlled by Rockefeller, *et al.*, the foundations and charities of Rockefeller *et al.* will generously fund progressive anti-capitalist /anti-war networks as well as environmentalists (opposed to Big Oil) with a view to ultimately overseeing and shaping their various activities. These mechanisms of "manufacturing dissent" require a manipulative environment, a process of arm-twisting and subtle cooptation of individuals within progressive organizations, including antiwar coalitions.

Whereas the mainstream media "manufactures consent", the complex network of NGOs (including segments of the alternative media) are used by the corporate elites to mould and manipulate the protest movement. In the US, the main antiwar coalitions, including United for Peace and Justice and MoveOn, are funded by the corporate establishment. Similarly, part of the "left leaning" alternative media, which has accepted the official 9/11 narrative, tends to pay lip service to the US-led war.[1]

At this juncture, "progressives" funded by major foundations are an obstacle to the formation of an articulate grassroots antiwar movement. A consistent antiwar movement must also confront various forms of cooption within its ranks, the fact that a significant sector of progressive opinion tacitly supports US foreign policy including "humanitarian interventions" under combined UN-NATO auspices.

An antiwar movement funded by major corporate foundations is the cause rather than the solution. A coherent antiwar movement cannot be funded by warmongers.

Jus ad Bellum: 9/11 and the Invasion of Afghanistan

The war on Afghanistan was upheld by several "progressives" as a "just war". The "self-defense" argument was accepted at face value as a legitimate response to the 9/11 attacks, without examining the fact that the US administration had not only supported the "Islamic terror network", it was also instrumental in the installation of the Taliban government in 1995-96.

In 2001, when Afghanistan was bombed and later invaded, "progressives" largely upheld the administration's "just cause" military doctrine. In the wake of 9/11, the antiwar movement against the illegal invasion of Afghanistan was isolated. The trade unions and civil society organizations had swallowed the media lies and government propaganda. They had accepted a war of retribution against Al Qaeda and the Taliban. Several prominent "left leaning" intellectuals upheld the "war on terrorism" agenda.

Media disinformation prevailed. People were misled as to the nature and objectives underlying the invasion of Afghanistan. Osama bin Laden and the Taliban were identified as the prime suspects of the 9/11 attacks, without a shred of evidence and without addressing the historical relationship between Al Qaeda and the US intelligence apparatus. In this regard, understanding 9/11 is crucial in formulating a consistent antiwar position. 9/11 is the pillar of US war propaganda; it sustains the illusion of an outside enemy, it justifies pre-emptive military intervention.

A meaningful anti-war movement requires breaking the "war on terrorism" and upholding 9/11 Truth. To reverse the tide of war and globalization requires a massive campaign of networking and outreach to inform people across the land, nationally and internationally, in neighborhoods, workplaces, parishes, schools, universities and municipalities, on the dangers of a US sponsored nuclear war.

The message should be loud and clear: Iran is not the threat. Even in the case of a conventional war (without the use of nukes), the proposed aerial bombardments could result in escalation, ultimately leading us into a broader war in the Middle East.

Debate and discussion must also take place within the military and intelligence community, particularly with regard to the use of tactical nuclear weapons, within the corridors of the US Congress, in municipalities and at all levels of government. Ultimately, the legitimacy of the political and military actors in high office must be challenged. The corporate media also bears a heavy responsibility for the cover-up of US-sponsored war crimes. It must also be forcefully challenged for its biased coverage of the Middle East war.

For the past year, Washington has been waging a "diplomatic arm twisting" exercise with a view to enlisting countries into supporting its military agenda. It is essential that at the diplomatic level, countries in the Middle East, Asia, Africa and Latin America take a firm stance against the US military agenda. Countries should opt out of the US-NATO military alliance, which also includes a number of non-NATO "partner countries".

Both Hillary Clinton and her predecessor at the State Department, Condoleezza Rice, have trekked across the Middle East, "expressing concern over Iran's nuclear program", seeking the unequivocal endorsement of the governments of the region against Tehran. Meanwhile both the Bush and Obama administrations have allocated funds in support of Iranian dissident groups both within Iran and the US.

Fake Antiwar Activism: Heralding Iran as a Nuclear Threat

Many people in the antiwar movement, while condemning the US administration, also condemn the government of President Ahmadinejad for its bellicose stance with regard to Israel. The *Jus ad Bellum* reasoning used as a pretext to bomb Yugoslavia on humanitarian grounds is now being applied to Iran. President Ahmadinejad allegedly wants Israel to be "wiped off the map" as first reported by the New York Times in October 2005:

Iran's conservative new president, Mahmoud Ahmadinejad, said... [on October 25, 2005] that Israel must be "wiped off the map" and that attacks by Palestinians would destroy it, the ISNA press agency reported.

Ahmadinejad was speaking to an audience of about 4,000 students at a program called "The World Without Zionism"... His tone was reminiscent of that of the early days of Iran's Islamic revolution in 1979. Iran and Israel have been bitter enemies since then, and anti-Israel slogans have been common at rallies.[2]

The alleged "Wiped off the Map" statement by Iran's president was never made. The rumor was fabricated by the American media with a view to discrediting Iran's head of state and providing a justification for waging an all out war on Iran:

On October 25th, 2005... the newly-elected Iranian President Mahmoud Ahmadinejad delivered a speech at a program, titled "The World Without Zionism".,.

Before we get to the infamous remark, it's important to note that the "quote" in question was itself a quote – they are the words of the late Ayatollah Khomeini, the father of the Islamic Revolution. Although he quoted Khomeini to affirm his own position on Zionism, the actual words belong to Khomeini and not Ahmadinejad. Thus, Ahmadinejad has essentially been credited (or blamed) for a quote that is not only unoriginal, but represents a viewpoint already in place well before he ever took office.

THE ACTUAL QUOTE:

So what did Ahmadinejad actually say? To quote his exact words in Farsi:

"Imam ghoft een rezhim-e ishghalgar-e qods bayad az safheh-ye ruzgar mahv shavad."

That passage will mean nothing to most people, but one word might ring a bell: rezhim-e. It is the word "regime", pronounced just like the English word with an extra "eh" sound at the end. Ahmadinejad did not refer to Israel the country or Israel the land mass, but the Israeli regime. This is a vastly significant distinction, as one cannot wipe a regime off the map.

Ahmadinejad does not even refer to Israel by name, he instead uses the specific phrase "rezhim-e ishghalgar-e qods" (regime occupying Jerusalem).

So this raises the question... What exactly did he want "wiped from the map"? The answer is: nothing. That's because the word "map" was never used. The Persian word for map, "nagsheh", is not contained anywhere in his original Farsi quote, or, for that matter, anywhere in his entire speech. Nor was the western phrase "wipe out" ever said. Yet we are led to believe that Iran's President threatened to "wipe Israel off the map", despite never having uttered the words "map", "wipe out" or even "Israel".

THE PROOF:

The full quote translated directly to English:

"The Imam said this regime occupying Jerusalem must vanish from the page of time."

Word by word translation:

Imam (Khomeini) ghoft (said) een (this) rezhim-e (regime) ishghalgar-e (occupying) qods (Jerusalem) bayad (must) az safheh-ye ruzgar (from page of time) mahv shavad (vanish from).[3]

What President Ahmadinejad was essentially calling for in his statement was *"regime change" in Tel Aviv.* Compare Ahmadinejad's bland statement on regime change in Israel with that of former Deputy Defense Secretary Paul Wolfowitz, who called for "ending states that sponsor terrorism". What Wolfowitz had in mind was the outright destruction of nation-states.

The alleged "Wiped off the Map" statement has served not only to justify a pre-emptive attack against Iran, but also to subdue and tame the antiwar movement. While the danger of an all-out war on Iran is a matter of concern, it is by no means a priority for the US, Canadian and European antiwar movements. In the US, there are very few antiwar events focusing on US-Israeli threats directed against Iran.[4]

On the other hand, there is an ongoing campaign led by *United Against Nuclear Iran (UANI),* calling on President Obama and the US Congress to prevent Iran from developing nuclear weapons. The

UANI collective, founded by Obama appointees Richard Holbrooke and Gary Samore, claims to be integrated by "human rights and humanitarian groups, the labor movement, political advocacy and grassroots organizations."[5]

> UANI's advisory board consists of a number of U.S. government insiders and big shots who have close ties with the U.S. statesmen including R. James Woolsey, the former head of CIA... By publishing propagandistic reports and articles on the purported hazard of Iran's nuclear activities, UANI also functions as a mouthpiece which is exclusively dedicated to fearmongering and spreading falsehood about Iran.[6]

Many people in the antiwar movement, while condemning the US, continue to believe that Iran constitutes a threat and that the solution is "regime change". The funding of NGOs (which are constituent members of major antiwar collectives) by tax exempt charities and corporate foundations, has also contributed to weakening antiwar activism in relation to Iran. Iran is viewed by many within the antiwar movement as a potential aggressor. Its non-existent nuclear weapons are considered a threat to global security.

The Road Ahead

What is required is the development of a broad-based grassroots network which seeks to disable patterns of authority and decision-making pertaining to war. This network would be established at all levels in society, towns and villages, workplaces, parishes. Trade unions, farmers' organizations, professional associations, business associations, student unions, veterans' associations and church groups would be called upon to integrate the antiwar organizational structure. Of crucial importance, this movement should extend into the armed forces as a means to breaking the legitimacy of war among servicemen and women.

The first task would be to disable war propaganda through an effective campaign against media disinformation. The corporate media would be directly challenged, leading to boycotts of major news outlets which are responsible for channeling disinformation into the news chain. This endeavor would require a parallel process at the grass roots level of sensitizing and educating fellow citizens on the nature of the war and the global crisis, as well as effectively "spreading the word" through advanced networking, through alternative media outlets on the internet, etc.

The creation of such a movement, which forcefully challenges the legitimacy of the structures of political authority, is no easy task. It requires a degree of solidarity, unity and commitment unparalleled in world history. It requires breaking down political and ideological barriers within society and acting with a single voice. It also requires eventually unseating the war criminals and indicting them for war crimes.

The Antiwar Movement within the State Structure and the Military

What are the countervailing forces which might prevent this war from occurring? There are numerous ongoing forces at work within the US State apparatus, the US Congress, the Pentagon and NATO. A broad debate should be initiated within the state system, the military, the intelligence agencies in the US and NATO countries. Public employees, including federal, state and municipal government officials, military and intelligence personnel at all levels must confront and challenge the authority of war criminals in high office: a "bureaucratic blockade" from within the state, by public sector employees at all levels must be implemented.

The hierarchy of political authority and decision making must be challenged and broken. Corruption and conflicts of interests must be revealed. "War is good for business": the financial interests behind this profit driven military must be fully understood. In other words, the powerful lobby groups which represent the interests of the weapons producers, the oil companies and Wall Street must be weakened from within.

The ongoing "war on terrorism" campaign involving the indoctrination of top officials in civilian government, the military, law enforcement, etc., must also be broken. The links between politicians and their corporate sponsors must be severed, with a view to restoring democratic forms of government. The war criminals in high office must lose their legitimacy in the eyes of public opinion. They must be recognized for what they are: war criminals. It is only when they lose their constituents and become politically isolated, that meaningful change can be carried out.

Abandon the Battlefield: Refuse to Fight

A coherent movement must be initiated within the armed forces in liaison with the broader antiwar movement. Members of the armed forces should disobey orders and refuse to participate in a criminal war. The military oath taken at the time of induction demands unbending support and allegiance to the US Constitution, while also demanding that US troops obey orders from their President and Commander in Chief:

> I, _____ , do solemnly swear (or affirm) that I will support and defend the Constitution of the United States against all enemies, foreign and domestic; that I will bear true faith and allegiance to the same; and that I will obey the orders of the President of the United States and the orders of the officers appointed over me, according to the regulations and the Uniform Code of Military Justice. So help me God.[7]

The President and Commander in Chief has blatantly violated all tenets of domestic and international law. So that making an oath to "obey orders from the President" is tantamount to violating rather than defending the US Constitution:

> The Uniform Code of Military Justice (UCMJ) 809.ART.90 (20), makes it clear that military personnel need to obey the "lawful command of his superior officer," 891.ART.91 (2), the "lawful order of a warrant officer", 892.ART.92 (1) the "lawful general order", 892.ART.92 (2) "lawful order". In each case, military personnel have an obligation and a duty to only obey Lawful orders and indeed have an obligation to disobey Unlawful orders, including orders by the president that do not comply with the UCMJ. The moral and legal obligation is to the U.S. Constitution and not to those who would issue un-

lawful orders, especially if those orders are in direct violation of the Constitution and the UCMJ.[8]

The Commander in Chief is a war criminal. According to Principle IV of the Nuremberg Tribunal:

> The fact that a person [e.g. Coalition troops] acted pursuant to order of his Government or of a superior does not relieve him from responsibility under international law, provided a moral choice was in fact possible to him.[9]

Let us make that "moral choice" possible to enlisted American, British, Canadian and coalition servicemen and women. Disobey unlawful orders! Abandon the battlefield! Refuse to fight in a war which blatantly violates international law and the US Constitution!

But this is not a choice which enlisted men and women can make individually. It is a collective and societal choice, which requires an organizational structure.

Across the land in the US, Britain, Canada and in all coalition countries, the antiwar movement must assist enlisted men and women to make that moral choice possible, to abandon the battlefield in Iraq and Afghanistan. This will not be an easy task. Committees at local levels must be set up across the United States, Canada, Britain, Italy, Japan and other countries, which have troops in Iraq and Afghanistan. We call upon veterans' associations and local communities to support this process.

This movement needs to dismantle the disinformation campaign. It must effectively reverse the indoctrination of coalition troops, who are led to believe that they are fighting "a just war": "a war against terrorists". The legitimacy of the US military authority must be broken.

The Broader Peace Process

People across the land, nationally and internationally, must mobilize against this diabolical military agenda, the authority of the state and its officials must be challenged.

This war can be prevented if people forcefully confront their governments, pressure their elected representatives, organize at the local level in towns, villages and municipalities, spread the word, inform their fellow citizens on the implications of a nuclear war, initiate debate and discussion within the armed forces.

The holding of mass demonstrations is not enough. What is required is the development of a broad and well-organized grassroots antiwar network which challenges the structures of power and authority, the nature of the economic system, the vast amounts of money used to fund the war, the sheer size of the so-called defense industry. What is required is a mass movement of people which forcefully challenges the legitimacy of war, a global people's movement which criminalizes war. What is needed *is to break the conspiracy of silence,* expose the media lies and distortions, and confront the criminal nature of the US Administration and of those governments which support it, its war agenda as well as its so-called "Homeland Security agenda" which has already defined the contours of a police state.

What Has to be Achieved

Reveal the criminal nature of this military project.

Break once and for all the lies and falsehoods which sustain the "political consensus" in favor of a pre-emptive nuclear war.

Undermine war propaganda, reveal the media lies, reverse the tide of disinformation, wage a consistent campaign against the corporate media.

Break the legitimacy of the warmongers in high office.

Dismantle the US-sponsored military adventure and its corporate sponsors.

Repeal the illusion that the state is committed to protecting its citizens.

Expose the "fake crises", such as the global flu pandemic, as a means to distract public opinion away from the dangers of a global war.

Uphold 9/11 Truth. Reveal the falsehoods behind 9/11 which are used to justify the Middle East/Central Asian war under the banner of the "Global War on Terrorism" (GWOT).

Expose how a profit-driven war serves the vested interests of the banks, the defense contractors, the oil giants, the media giants and the biotech conglomerates.

Challenge the corporate media which deliberately obfuscates the causes and consequences of this war.

Reveal and take cognizance of the unspoken and tragic outcome of a war waged with nuclear weapons.

Call for the Dismantling of NATO.

Implement the prosecution of war criminals in high office.

Close down the weapons assembly plants and implement the foreclosure of major weapons producers.

Close down all US military bases in the US and around the world.

Develop an antiwar movement within the armed forces and establish bridges between the armed forces and the civilian antiwar movement.

Forcefully pressure governments of both NATO and non-NATO countries to withdraw from the US-led global military agenda.

Develop a consistent antiwar movement in Israel. Inform the citizens of Israel of the likely consequences of a US-NATO-Israeli attack on Iran.

Target the pro-war lobby groups including the pro-Israeli groups in the US.

Dismantle the homeland security state, call for the repeal of the PATRIOT legislation.

The world is at the crossroads of the most serious crisis in modern history. The US has embarked on a military adventure, "a long war", which threatens the future of humanity. It is essential to bring the US war project to the forefront of political debate, particularly in North America and Western Europe. Political and military leaders who are opposed to the war must take a firm stance, from within their respective institutions. Citizens must take a stance individually and collectively against war.

This war is sheer madness. World War III is terminal.

Albert Einstein understood the perils of nuclear war and the extinction of life on earth, which has already started with the radioactive contamination resulting from depleted uranium. *"I know not with what weapons World War III will be fought, but World War IV will be fought with sticks and stones."*

The media, the intellectuals, the scientists and the politicians, in chorus, obfuscate the untold truth, namely that war using nuclear warheads destroys humanity, and that this complex process of gradual destruction has already commenced.

When the lie becomes the truth, there is no turning backwards.

When war is upheld as a humanitarian endeavor, justice and the entire international legal system are turned upside down: pacifism and the antiwar movement are criminalized. Opposing the war becomes a criminal act.

The lie must be exposed for what it is and what it does:

It sanctions the indiscriminate killing of men, women and children. It destroys families and people.

It destroys the commitment of people towards their fellow human beings.

It prevents people from expressing their solidarity for those who suffer. It upholds war and the police state as the sole avenue. It destroys both nationalism and internationalism.

Breaking the lie means breaking a criminal project of global destruction, in which the quest for profit is the overriding force.

This profit-driven military agenda destroys human values and transforms people into unconscious zombies.

Let us reverse the tide.

Challenge the war criminals in high office and the powerful corporate lobby groups which support them.

Break the American Inquisition.

Undermine the US-NATO-Israel military crusade.

Close down the weapons factories and the military bases.

Members of the armed forces should disobey orders and refuse to participate in a criminal war.

Bring home the troops.

NOTES

1. Michel Chossudovsky, "'Manufacturing Dissent': The Anti-Globalization Movement is Funded by the Corporate Elites", *Global Research,* http://globalresearch.ca/index.php?context=va&aid=21110, 20 September 2010.

2. Nazila Fathi, "Wipe Israel 'off the map' Iranian says", *The New York Times,* http://www.nytimes.com/2005/10/26/world/africa/26iht-iran.html?_r=1, 27 October 2005.

3. See the detailed article by Arash Norouzi, "Israel: 'Wiped off The Map'. The Rumor of the Century, Fabricated by the US Media to Justify an All-Out War on Iran", *Global*

Research, http://www.globalresearch.ca/index.php?context=va&aid=21188, 20 February 2007. The full transcript of the speech in Farsi is archived on Ahmadinejad's web site: www.president.ir/farsi/ahmadinejad/speeches/1384/aban-84/840804sahyonizm.htm

4. See main US anti-war collective, United for Peace & Justice, http://www.unitedfor peace.org/, "United for Peace & Justice : Events" at http://webcache.googleusercon tent.com/search?q=cache:ZVZriqdwWdkJ:www.unitedforpeace.org/calendar+antiwar+i ran+UFPJ&cd=5&hl=en&ct=clnk&gl=ca.

5. United Against Nuclear Iran (UANI), "Coalition Information", http://www.uniteda gainstnucleariran.com/about/coalition.

6. Orwell's Dreams, "Spreading falsehoods about Iran: 'United Against Nuclear Iran': America's war propaganda mouthpiece", *Orwell's Dreams,* 20 September 2010, http://or wellsdreams.wordpress.com/2010/09/20/spreading-falsehoods-about-iran-united-againstnuclear-iran-americas-war-propaganda-mouthpiece/.

7. Armed Services, Oath of Enlistment, Title 10, US Code; Act of May 5, 1960 replacing the wording first adopted in 1789, with amendment effective October 5, 1962. The "Oath of Enlistment" into the United States Armed Forces is performed upon any person enlisting or re-enlisting for a term of service into any branch of the military.

8. Lawrence Mosqueda, "An Advisory to US Troops: A Duty to Disobey All Unlawful Orders", *Global Research,* http://globalresearch.ca/articles/MOS303A.html, 2 March 2003. See also Michel Chossudovsky, "'We the People Refuse to Fight': Abandon the Battlefield!", *Global Research*, http://www.globalresearch.ca/index.php?context= va&aid=2130, 18 March 2006.

9. See "Principles of the Nuremberg Tribunal", 1950, http://deoxy.org/wc/wc-nurem.htm.

GLOBAL RESEARCH PUBLISHERS

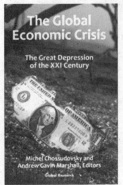

The Global Economic Crisis:
The Great Depression of the XXI Century
MICHEL CHOSSUDOVSKY AND ANDREW GAVIN
MARSHALL, EDITORS
ISBN 978-0973714739 (2010), 416 pages
    In all major regions of the world, the economic recession is deep-seated, resulting in mass unemployment, the collapse of state social programs and the impoverishment of millions of people. The meltdown of financial markets was the result of institutionalized fraud and financial manipulation. The economic crisis is accompanied by a worldwide process of militarization, a "war without borders" led by the U.S. and its NATO allies.

This book takes the reader through the corridors of the Federal Reserve, into the plush corporate boardrooms on Wall Street where far-reaching financial transactions are routinely undertaken.

Each of the authors in this timely collection digs beneath the gilded surface to reveal a complex web of deceit and media distortion which serves to conceal the workings of the global economic system and its devastating impacts on people's lives.

The Globalization of Poverty
and the New World Order
MICHEL CHOSSUDOVSKY
ISBN 09737147-0-0 (2003), 403 pages
In this new and expanded edition of Chossudovsky's international best-seller, the author outlines the contours of a New World Order which feeds on human poverty and the destruction of the environment, generates social apartheid, encourages racism and ethnic strife and undermines the rights of women. The result as his detailed examples from all parts of the world show so convincingly, is a globalization of poverty.

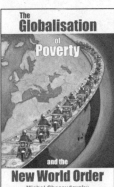

This book is a skilful combination of lucid explanation and cogently argued critique of the fundamentaldirections in which our world is moving financially and economically.

In this new enlarged edition –which includes ten new chapters and a new introduction- the author reviews the causes and consequences of famine in Sub-Saharan Africa, the dramatic meltdown of financial markets, the demise of State social programs and the devastation resulting from corporate downsizing and trade liberalization.

Award winning author and economics professor Michel Chossudovsky is Director of the Centre for Research on Globalization (CRG).

••• For prices and ordering details, visit our online store •••

Seeds of Destruction:
The Hidden Agenda of Genetic Manipulation
F. WILLIAM ENGDAHL
ISBN 978-0-937147-2-2 (2007), 341 pages

This skillfully researched book focuses on how a small socio-political American elite seeks to establish control over the very basis of human survival: the provision of our daily bread. *"Control the food and you control the people."*

This is no ordinary book about the perils of GMO. Engdahl takes the reader inside the corridors of power, into the backrooms of the science labs, behind closed doors in the corporate boardrooms.

The author cogently reveals a diabolical World of profit-driven political intrigue, government corruption and coercion, where genetic manipulation and the patenting of life forms are used to gain worldwide control over food production. If the book often reads as a crime story, that should come as no surprise. For that is what it is.

Engdahl's carefully argued critique goes far beyond the familiar controversies surrounding the practice of genetic modification as a scientific technique. The book is an eye-opener, a must-read for all those committed to the causes of social justice and world peace.

F. William Engdahl is a leading analyst of the New World Order, author of the best-selling book on oil and geopolitics, A Century of War: Anglo-American Politics and the New World Order.

America's "War on Terrorism"
MICHEL CHOSSUDOVSKY
ISBN 0-9737147-1-9 (2005), 387 pages

In this 2005 best-selling title, the author blows away the smokescreen put up by the mainstream media, that 9/11 was an attack on America by "Islamic terrorists". Through meticulous research, the author uncovers a military-intelligence ploy behind the September 11 attacks, and the cover-up and complicity of key members of the Bush Administration.

This expanded edition, which includes twelve new chapters, focuses on the use of 9/11 as a pretext for the invasion and illegal occupation of Iraq, the militarization of justice and law enforcement and the repeal of democracy.

According to Chossudovsky, the "war on terrorism" is a complete fabrication based on the illusion that one man, Osama bin Laden, outwitted the $40 billion-a-year American intelligence apparatus. The "war on terrorism" is a war of conquest. Globalization is the final march to the "New World Order", dominated by Wall Street and the U.S. military-industrial complex.

September 11, 2001 provides a justification for waging a war without borders. Washington's agenda consists in extending the frontiers of the American Empire to facilitate complete U.S. corporate control, while installing within America the institutions of the Homeland Security State. Chossudovsky peels back layers of rhetoric to reveal a complex web of deceit aimed at luring the American people and the rest of the world into accepting a military solution which threatens the future of humanity.